Implementing XML: Managing and formatting data

Copyright - Editions ENI - September 2001
ISBN: 2-7460-1349-5
Original edition: 2-7460-1285-5

Editions ENI

BP 32125
44021 NANTES Cedex 1

Tél. : 02.51.80.15.15
Fax : 02.51.80.15.16

e-mail : editions@ediENI.com
http://www.editions-eni.com

Collection directed by Joëlle MUSSET
English edition by Andrew BLACKBURN

Introduction

Chapter 1

XML syntax

Chapter 2

DTD (Document Type Declaration) Chapter 3

Style sheets Chapter 4

XPath

Chapter 5

Developing

Chapter 6

New standards

Chapter 7

Appendices

Chapter 1: Introduction

This book describes how you can implement and use XML.

This book does not aim to teach you to use any specific application.

Before reading this book, you need to have a basic understanding of some server-side Internet development language concepts, such as ASP *(Active Server Page)*, style sheets, JavaScript and HTML *(HyperText Markup Language)*.

To view XML *(eXtensible Markup Language)* you need a parser. A parser is a document analyser. From its version 5, the Microsoft Internet Explorer browser includes the MSXML parser. At the time of writing, the current version of MSXML was MSXML 3.

Most of the examples in this book were carried out in a Microsoft environment.

A. History of XML

The forerunner of all Internet development languages was SGML. IBM was one of the first organizations to support SGML, which it used for text entry and formatting.

HTML is the best-known markup language and was also the first Internet development language. Today, HTML has become the Internet development standard.

HTML is easy to use. It offers a large number of tools that allow you either to write directly in HTML or to convert an existing document into HTML, with a simple **Save As** command.

In fact, HTML was not designed for use with complex applications. Its sole objective was to publish information on the Internet.

You can use a number of other languages with HTML to extend its features.

Today however, the needs of the Internet user are changing and this is where XML comes in.

B. SGML and HTML

1. SGML

SGML *(Standard Generalized Markup Language)* appeared in 1986 as the first electronic document standard.

SGML includes three basic items. These items are different for each SGML application:

- **DTD** *(Document Type Definition)*: the DTD defines the structure of the document.

– **Document instance**: this is the document text. It includes the SGML elements the DTD defines to identify the different parts of the text. A document instance can share a DTD with other document instances. However, a document instance must conform to one DTD only.

– **Document summary**: the document summary defines the main features of the SGML application. These features include the chosen options and character set.

SGML is difficult to use. Setting up an Internet application with SGML requires a lot of tools and a lot of time.

To make SGML more portable and simpler to use on the Internet, the HTML application was developed using the SGML language.

2. HTML

As noted above, HTML has become the standard for Web development.

HTML is simple to use. A single HTML document contains both the text that must be displayed and the instructions indicating how the text must be displayed. A large number of applications allow you to create HTML documents. These applications range from simple text editors such as **Vi** on **Linux**, **Edit** on **MS-DOS** and **Notepad** on **Windows**, to WYSIWYG *(What You See Is What You Get)* applications, such as **Microsoft FrontPage** for the home user and **Microsoft Visual Interdev** and **Macromedia Dreamweaver** for the professional user.

Concerning the syntax checking, as an SGML application, HTML is associated with a DTD. There is one DTD for each version of HTML. The W3C *(World Wide Web Consortium)* Internet site includes the DTD for HTML version 4: **DTD HTML 4.0 Transitional**.

⊚ The W3C groups together all the technologies that allow you to use all the features of the Web.

One drawback of HTML is its static syntax. Unlike DHTML, HTML does not allow you to add custom tags, as it was not designed for this purpose.

Above all, HTML was designed to allow large numbers of Internet authors to publish their documents as simply as possible. Indeed, HTML fulfills this function very well. On the other hand, most of today's Internet content is defined by the limits of HTML.

C. XML

XML is derived from SGML. It aims to offer the best of HTML and of SGML.

The XML designers have included only the features you need for Web applications. As a measure of language complexity, the XML specification covers only 35 pages, as opposed to 155 pages for the SGML application.

XML must be compatible with SGML.

The most important feature in common with SGML is that each XML document can be based on a DTD. However, an XML document does not have to be associated with a DTD (cf. Chapter 3: Declaring the type of document).

In an XML document, the format of the information is separated from the text itself.

XML was originally developed for the Internet. However, as you can associate different DTDs with your XML document, you can use XML with different applications, as a means of data exchange or storage.

In fact, it is even easier to write with XML than it is to write with its predecessor, HTML. With HTML, you need to know the different tags and how you can use them, whereas with XML you can simply create your tags as and when you need them. This approach means that anyone can understand the text of an XML document.

Unlike HTML, XML separates the data presentation from its content. You can associate several formats with the same content. This approach allows you to display your XML according to your needs (as a table, as a chart or as part of a picture, for example).

```
<?xml version="1.0"?>
<AUCTIONBLOCK>

  <ITEM>
    <TITLE>Vase and Stones</TITLE>
    <ARTIST>Linda Mann</ARTIST>
    <DIMENSIONS>20x30 inches</DIMENSIONS>
    <MATERIALS>oil</MATERIALS>
    <YEAR>1996</YEAR>
    <DESCRIPTION>Still Life</DESCRIPTION>
    <PREVIEW-SMALL src="burl-s.jpg" width="300"
height="194" alt="Vase and Stones"/>
    <BIDS>
      <BID>
        <PRICE>6000</PRICE>
        <TIME>3:02:22 PM</TIME>
        <BIDDER>Chris</BIDDER>
        <TIMESTAMP>1307</TIMESTAMP>
      </BID>
      <BID>
        <PRICE>5700</PRICE>
        <TIME>2:58:42 PM</TIME>
        <BIDDER>John</BIDDER>
        <TIMESTAMP>1315</TIMESTAMP>
      </BID>
      <BID>
        <PRICE>5600</PRICE>
        <TIME>2:54:32 PM</TIME>
        <BIDDER>Andrew</BIDDER>
        <TIMESTAMP>1308</TIMESTAMP>
      </BID>
      <BID>
        <PRICE>5500</PRICE>
        <TIME>2:48:08 PM</TIME>
        <BIDDER>Chris</BIDDER>
        <TIMESTAMP>1307</TIMESTAMP>
      </BID>
      <BID>
        <PRICE>5000</PRICE>
        <TIME>2:47:58 PM</TIME>
        <BIDDER>opening price</BIDDER>
        <TIMESTAMP>1298</TIMESTAMP>
```

table.xsl →

Price	Time	Bidder
$6000	3:02:22 PM	Chris
$5700	2:58:42 PM	John
$5600	2:54:32 PM	Andrew
$5500	2:48:08 PM	Chris
$5000	2:47:58 PM	opening price

bar.xsl →

Vase and Stones by Linda Mann

Chris (3:02 PM)	$6000
John (2:58 PM)	$5700
Andrew (2:54 PM)	$5600
Chris (2:48 PM)	$5500
$5000 opening price (2:47 PM)	

art.xsl →

An XML document can have several target devices:

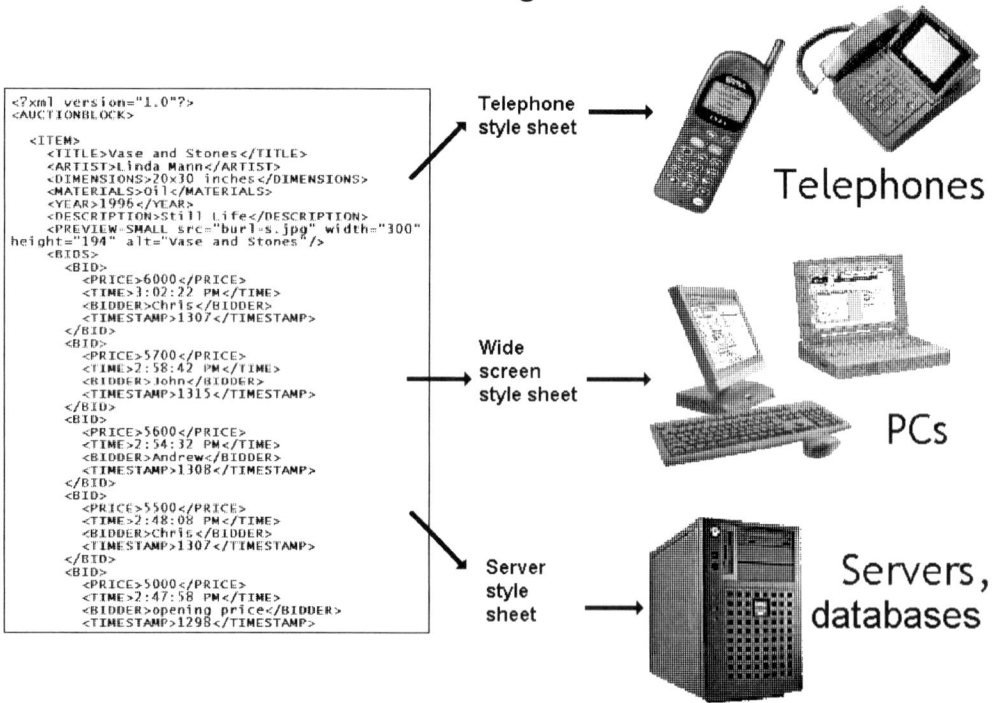

```
<?xml version="1.0"?>
<AUCTIONBLOCK>

   <ITEM>
      <TITLE>Vase and Stones</TITLE>
      <ARTIST>Linda Mann</ARTIST>
      <DIMENSIONS>20x30 inches</DIMENSIONS>
      <MATERIALS>Oil</MATERIALS>
      <YEAR>1996</YEAR>
      <DESCRIPTION>Still Life</DESCRIPTION>
      <PREVIEW-SMALL src="burl-s.jpg" width="300"
height="194" alt="Vase and Stones"/>
      <BIDS>
         <BID>
            <PRICE>6000</PRICE>
            <TIME>3:02:22 PM</TIME>
            <BIDDER>Chris</BIDDER>
            <TIMESTAMP>1307</TIMESTAMP>
         </BID>
         <BID>
            <PRICE>5700</PRICE>
            <TIME>2:58:42 PM</TIME>
            <BIDDER>john</BIDDER>
            <TIMESTAMP>1315</TIMESTAMP>
         </BID>
         <BID>
            <PRICE>5600</PRICE>
            <TIME>2:54:32 PM</TIME>
            <BIDDER>Andrew</BIDDER>
            <TIMESTAMP>1308</TIMESTAMP>
         </BID>
         <BID>
            <PRICE>5500</PRICE>
            <TIME>2:48:08 PM</TIME>
            <BIDDER>Chris</BIDDER>
            <TIMESTAMP>1307</TIMESTAMP>
         </BID>
         <BID>
            <PRICE>5000</PRICE>
            <TIME>2:47:58 PM</TIME>
            <BIDDER>opening price</BIDDER>
            <TIMESTAMP>1298</TIMESTAMP>
```

Telephone style sheet → **Telephones**

Wide screen style sheet → **PCs**

Server style sheet → **Servers, databases**

You can also sort your data, automatically generate tables of contents and use many other features.

Here is a common use of XML:

Many Microsoft "2000", XP or **.net** tools support XML.

Save a Word 2000 document as a Web page (by selecting the **File - Save as Web Page** menu option). Open your Explorer and select the HTML document you have just created. Right-click this document and choose **Edit**. Your document should appear alone in the Word application. If you carry out the same operation with an Excel file, it will appear in the Excel application. But, how can a simple HTML file know which application created it? To answer this question, close the Word application and open this HTML file with a text editor, such as Notepad (right-click the file and choose **Open With - Choose Program - Notepad**).

When you save your file in HTML format, the Word (or Excel etc.) application includes XML statements specifying the original application as the default editing program. These statements are delimited by the **<XML>** ... **</XML>** tags.

Installing MSXML3

To install MSXML3 you need to download the **msxml3.exe** file from the Microsoft site. If your machine does not run any 2000-version Microsoft product, you must first install the MSI *(Microsoft Installer)*, which you can also download from the Microsoft site. You may have some conflict problems if your machine runs MSXML2, which Internet Explorer 4 provides. In this case, MSXML3 will be installed with MSXML2 in side-by-side mode. You can use the **xmlinst.exe** utility to delete the MSXML2 entries from the registry database and allow MSXML3 to run alone (you can also download **xmlinst.exe** from the Microsoft site: if you download **xmlinst** as a compressed file, you must first decompress it then run the **xmlinst.exe** program).

D.Tagging

As with SGML and HTML, XML is a tagging language.

The term tagging comes from the printing industry where tags were added to a text sequence, to provide additional instructions for reworking the document later.

For electronic documents, electronic tagging allows applications to extract the data and rework it.

The purpose of tagging is to allow an application to format the document. One of the best-known text formats is RTF *(Rich Text Format)*.

Here is an example of the famous "Hello World!" sentence in RTF. In this case "World" has been written in a bold Verdana font.

RTF version

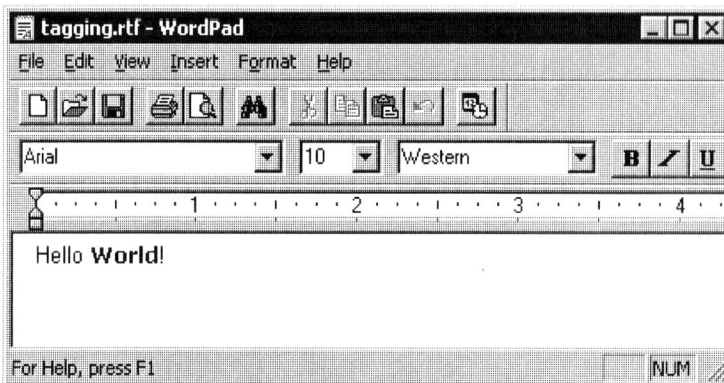

RTF source:

```
{\rtf1\ansi\ansicpg1252\deff0\deflang1033
{\fonttbl
{\f0\fswiss\fcharset0 Arial;}
{\f1\fswiss\fprq2\fcharset0 Verdana;}
}
\viewkind4\uc1\pard\f0\fs20 Hello \b\f1 World\b0\f0 !\par
}
```

To view the RTF source on Windows, you can open your RTF file using the Notepad editor.

Although this code may seem complex at first sight, closer analysis allows you to identify certain elements:

– The first part is the document header, which defines the fonts used.
– The next part is the body of the document. The document body refers to the font definitions \f0 and \f1 and contains the document text. Notice the bold sequence: the word "World" appears between the \b ... \b0 tags.

Each of these tags serves a purpose.

The rest of this chapter examines the same text in HTML and in XML.

HTML version

As seen in a browser:

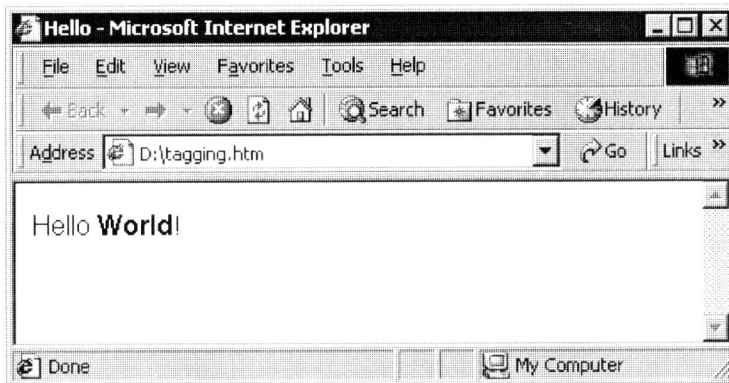

HTML source:

```
<html>
  <head>
    <title>Hello</title>
  </head>
  <body>
    <font face="arial">Hello <fontface="verdana"><b>world</b></font>!
    </font>
  </body>
</html>
```

To view the HTML source on Windows, you can open your HTML file using the Notepad editor. The structure of this HTML document is much simpler than that of the RTF version.

As with XML, all HTML tags start with a < and end with a >.

An element is composed of an **opening tag** (for example, <html>), a tag content and a **closing tag** (for example, </html>).

This document begins with an **<html>** tag and ends with a **</html>** tag. This element is called the document element.

Next comes the HTML header, delimited by the **<head>...</head>** tags.

This header contains the title element. The title element is composed of the **<title> ... </title>** tags, delimiting the title text: "Hello" in this case.

The body of the document follows the header. The **<body> ... </body>** tags delimit the body element. HTML covers all aspects of the document. As with RTF, HTML specifies the fonts that are used (with the **<font face ...">** ... **</font>** tags), the text "Hello World!" and the bold formatting of the word "World" (with the **<b> ... </b>** tags).

At the end of the document, the **</body>** tag and the **</html>** tag close these two elements.

Implementing XML

Notice that the HTML format is quite different from the RTF format.

Here is the XML format:

XML version

As seen in a browser:

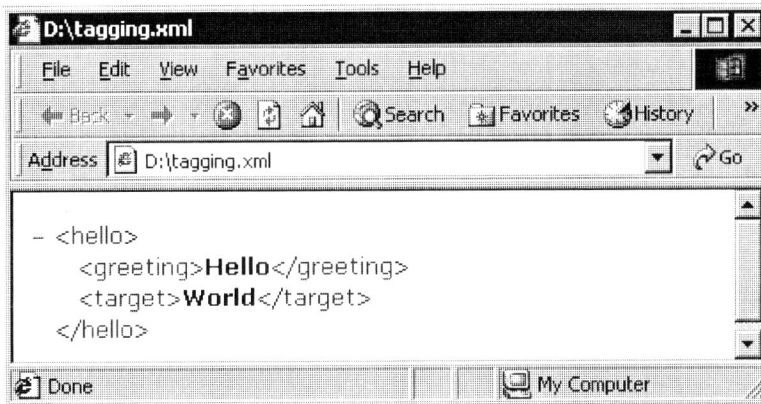

```
D:\tagging.xml                                    _ □ ×
 File   Edit   View   Favorites   Tools   Help
 ← Back  -  →  -  ⊗  ⚡  ⌂  | ⊗ Search  ⊞ Favorites  ⊛ History   »
 Address  📄 D:\tagging.xml                            ▼  ⤳ Go

  − <hello>
       <greeting>Hello</greeting>
       <target>World</target>
    </hello>

 📄 Done                               🖳 My Computer
```

XML source:

```
<hello>
  <greeting>Hello</greeting>
  <target>world</target>
</hello>
```

The XML source code for this document does not look much like the RTF source code at all. In this XML source, the **<hello> ... </hello>** tags de-limit the document element (to use HTML terminology). The document ele-ment accommodates the "greeting" element and the "target" element, which contain "Hello" and "World" respectively.

That is all this document contains: there is no formatting information and even the "!" is absent.

You can specify all this information when you create the associated format-ting file.

Managing and formatting data

Chapter 2: XML syntax

The XML structure is easy to declare and validate.

Furthermore, XML combines the flexibility of SGML with the simplicity of HTML.

A. Structure of an XML document

An XML document contains elements, tags and various attribute and comments blocks. It includes comments, as in HTML and a DTD, as in SGML.

⚙ XML is case sensitive.

Here is an example of XML source code:

```
<!-- Prolog -->
<?xml version ="1.0" encoding="UTF-8" ?>
<!DOCTYPE cd.list SYSTEM "cd_list.dtd">
<!-- Document element -->
<cd.list>
<!-- First child -->
  <cd>
  <!-- Artist child element -->
    <artist>Keith Jarrett</artist>
  <!-- Title child element -->
    <title>The Koln Concert</title>
  <!-- Specification child element -->
  <!-- Attributes: type and number of CDs -->
    <spec type="Live" nb_cd="1" />
  </cd>
<!-- Second child -->
  <cd>
    <artist>Keith Jarrett</artist>
    <title>La Scala</title>
    <spec type="Live" nb_cd="1" />
  </cd>
</cd.list>
```

> To test this example, copy the lines from **<?xml version ...?>** to **</cd.list>** inclusive into Notepad, omitting the line **<!DOCTYPE ... >**. Record this document with an **.xml** name extension and open it using Internet Explorer 5 (or later version).

This example concerns a list of audio CDs. This type of document is relatively easy to understand.

Here is this XML code in Internet Explorer:

Internet Explorer highlights the different parts of the document. By clicking the minus (-) or the plus (+) signs you can collapse or expand the different elements in the tree.

All XML documents include a **prolog**, a **document element** and a **tree**. The tree contains nested elements (with parent/child relationships) and adjacent elements.

The prolog appears at the beginning of the document. In this example, the prolog is composed of an XML declaration and a document type declaration.

The **cd.list** element is the document element. The **cd.list** element is composed of two **cd** elements. Each **cd** element has the same structure: an **artist** element, a **title** element and a **spec** element. The **spec** element has two attributes: a **type** attribute and an **nb_cd** attribute.

Even though this code is simple to understand, a browser still makes it easier to spot any errors.

B. Prolog

The prolog can contain the XML declaration, processing instructions and a document type declaration.

1. XML declaration

The XML declaration is one of the processing instructions, in fact.

Here is an example of an XML declaration:

```
<?xml version="1.0" encoding="ISO-8859-1" standalone="yes" ?>
```

This declaration can provide three types of information:

version

> the version of XML that the document uses (version 1.0 in the example above).

encoding

> the character set that the document uses: the standard character set for Western Europe is **ISO-8859-1**. By default, the **encoding** attribute is set to the value **UTF8**.

standalone

> indicates the dependency of the document with respect to a document type declaration. If you set **standalone** to **yes**, the application processor does not seek any document type declaration outside the document. Otherwise, the application processor will be expecting an external document type declaration.

Although the XML declaration is optional, it is advisable to make one.

If you include this declaration, it must appear on the first line of your XML document and you must declare the **version**, **encoding** and **standalone** attributes in this order.

2. Processing instructions

The application processor interprets the processing instructions.

The most common processing instructions are the XML declaration (see above) and the style sheet declaration.

A processing instruction has the following format:

```
<?application "argument1" "argument2" ... ?>
```

The applications that generate XML code often create these instructions. Suppose you have a database server that needs to transfer information to a processing application (such as an invoicing program). The database server could pass this information to this application, as arguments via processing instructions.

The **xml** keyword is reserved. It can be in uppercase or lowercase characters. You can use this keyword for an XML declaration or a style sheet declaration.

Here is an example of a style sheet declaration:

```
<?xml-stylesheet type="text/xsl" href=" cd_list.xsl"?>
```

In this example, the application is **xml-stylesheet**, the XML style sheet processor. You can use two types of style sheet: XSL style sheets, which are specific to XML and CSS style sheets, which appeared with HTML. The **type** attribute indicates the file type (**text/css** for CSS style sheets) and the **href** attribute indicates the file's location.

3. Document type declaration (DTD)

When present, this declaration indicates the structure of the document. The DTD can refer to an external subset or an internal subset or both.

Here is an example of a Document Type Declaration (DTD):

```
<!DOCTYPE cd.list SYSTEM "cd_list.dtd">
```

This DTD refers to an external subset (cf. Chapter 3.A - Types of DTD).

The DTD defines the root element (**cd.list** in this example) and the name of the file that contains the document structure (**cd_list.dtd** in this example).

◉ Although the DTD is optional, it is advisable to include one, as it helps you to validate your document. Chapter 3 describes DTDs in greater detail.

C. Comments

XML uses the same comments tag syntax as HTML. A comments tag begins with **<!--** and ends with **-->**. You can include a comment anywhere, provided it is not inside another tag.

Here is an example of a valid comments tag:

```
<elem> text <!-- this is correct --> text </elem>
```

Here is an example of an invalid comments tag:

```
<elem <!-- this is not correct --> > text </elem>
```

◉ You cannot include the string "--" in a comment.

D.Element tree

All XML documents represent an element tree. As with all trees, element trees have a root, branches and leaves: in this case, in the form of elements.

⮞ When you name your elements, you must respect certain rules. A name must never begin with a digit. If the name comprises a single character, it must be an alphabetic character ("a" to "z" or "A" to "Z"); otherwise, the first character can also be an underscore (_) or a colon (:). Subsequent characters can be letters, digits, hyphens (-), underscores (_) or periods (.).

Here is an example of an element tree:

```
<list.cd>
   <cd>
       <artist>Keith Jarrett</artist>
       <title>The Koln Concert</title>
       <spec type="Live" nb_cd="1" />
   </cd>
   <cd>
       <artist>Keith Jarrett</artist>
       <title>La Scala</title>
       <spec type="Live" nb_cd="1"/>
   </cd>
</List.cd>
```

1. Document element

Every XML document has only one document element. This element encapsulates all the subsequent items, whether they are elements, texts, attributes, entities or CDATA sections.

In the above example, the document element is:

```
<list.cd> ... </list.cd>
```

2. Elements

The elements are the main components of the document. An element can contain text or other elements. When an element contains other elements, the contained elements are called **child elements**.

Here is an example of an element that contains text:

```
<artist>Keith Jarrett</artist>
```

Here is an example of an element that contains other elements:

```
<cd>
      <artist>Keith Jarrett</artist>
      <title>The Koln Concert</title>
      <spec type="Live" nb_cd="1" />
</cd>
```

3. Attributes

An element can contain one or more attributes. An element must not contain the same element twice: otherwise, the document is said to be "not well formed". Chapter 3: DTD *(Document Type Declaration)* discusses the "well formed" concept in greater detail.

An attribute is composed of a name and a value. You cannot include an attribute in the opening tag of an element. When you name your attributes, you must follow the same rules as for elements (see the **Element tree** section, above).

Here is an example of an element that contains an attribute:

```
<contact company = "ENI Publishing">
      Andrew Blackburn
</contact>
```

Here is an example of an element that does not contain any attributes:

```
<spec type="Live" nb_cd="1" />
```

4. Entities

Entities can be definable or they can be predefined. They can also be internal or external.

You must declare your entities within the DTD, using the **ENTITY** keyword. On the other hand, you can use attributes in the DTD or in the XML document.

Some entities are predefined. This approach allows you to display characters such as < or >.

Here is an example of an entity declaration:

```
<!ENTITY hi "Hello World!">
```

This example defines the **hi** entity as being equivalent to the text sequence "Hello World!".

You can use an entity as follows:

```
<element>&hi;</element>
```

5. CDATA sections

A CDATA section can contain practically any character sequence. CDATA sections allow you to display blocks of characters that the XML processor must not parse. You can use a CDATA section to show code sequence examples as text blocks, for example.

Here is an example of a CDATA section:

```
<![CDATA[Welcome to this <XML> page]]>
```

The only characters you cannot include in a CDATA section are]] (the characters that close the section). Consequently, you cannot include a CDATA section within another CDATA section.

Chapter 3: DTD (Document Type Declaration)

A document type declaration can include element declarations, attribute declarations, entity declarations, notation declarations and comments.

The naming rules for these items are the same as those for XML elements, as set out in the "Element tree" section of Chapter 2: XML syntax.

A. Types of DTD

Your DTD can be **internal** or **external** or both. An internal DTD is an integral part of the XML document. On the other hand, an external DTD resides in a separate file, which allows you to use it for several XML documents. You can separate an external DTD into two categories: **private** (or **system**) or **public**. You must access a private DTD locally, whereas anyone can access a public DTD via a URI *(Uniform Resource Identifier)*.

```
<!DOCTYPE doc.element declarations>
```

You can use the declarations in this example only in the element tree whose document element is **doc.element**.

Finally, you can combine both internal and external declarations, as a **mixed** DTD.

An internal DTD can have the same contents as an external DTD. The only difference between the two is that an internal DTD appears inside your XML document as part of the prolog, whereas an external DTD appears in its own file.

Here is an example of a declaration in an internal DTD:

```
<!DOCTYPE cd.list [
   <!ELEMENT cd.list (cd)*>
   <!ELEMENT cd (artist, title, spec)>
   <!ELEMENT artist (#PCDATA)>
   <!ELEMENT title (#PCDATA)>
   <!ELEMENT spec (#PCDATA)>
   <!ATTLIST spec
      type (Sound_track | Live | Compilation) #IMPLIED
      nb_cd CDATA "1"
   >
]>
```

An external DTD can contain two types of declaration: private or public. A private declaration contains the **SYSTEM** keyword, which indicates a file on the local computer for private access only. A public declaration contains the **PUBLIC** keyword, which indicates a file on a Web server that anyone can access.

Here is an example of a **SYSTEM** declaration in an external DTD:

```
<!DOCTYPE cd.list SYSTEM "cd_list.dtd">
```

Here is the associated file:

```
<?xml version="1.0" encoding="UTF-8"?>
<!ELEMENT cd.list (cd+)>
<!ELEMENT cd (artist, title, spec)>
<!ELEMENT artist (#PCDATA)>
<!ELEMENT title (#PCDATA)>
<!ELEMENT spec (#PCDATA)>
<!ATTLIST spec
   type (Sound_track | Live | Compilation) #IMPLIED
   nb_cd CDATA "1"
>
```

Here is an example of a mixed DTD declaration:

```
<!DOCTYPE cd.list SYSTEM "cd_list.dtd" [
     <!ENTITY KJ "Keith Jarrett">
]>
```

This declaration adds the **KJ** entity to the external declaration.

Here is an example of a **PUBLIC** declaration in an external DTD:

```
<!DOCTYPE svg PUBLIC "-//W3C//DTD SVG 20001102//EN"
"http://www.w3.org/TR/2000/CR-SVG-20001102/DTD/svg-
20001102.dtd">
```

An FPI *(Formal Public Identifier)* follows the **PUBLIC** keyword.

Here is the format of an FPI:
type//owner//class description//language
A URL can appear after an FPI, to indicate where the DTD resides.

The **type** guarantees the uniqueness of the FPI identifier. To ensure it's uniqueness, you must register your FPI, which must comply with the ISO 9070 standard.

The **owner** specifies the owner of the FPI.

The **class** indicates the class of the document text.

Finally, the FPI contains a **description** of the document text and the **language** the document uses.

The above example shows a non-registered FPI owned by the W3C. The document's text class is DTD. The document concerns SVG, it is dated 02/11/2000 and is written in English.

⊙ SVG *(Scalable Vector Graphics)*: cf. section A.1 of Chapter 7 - New Standards.

B. Element declarations

Here is the format of an element declaration:

```
<!ELEMENT elt.name elt.type>
```

The **elt.name** is the name of the element and the **elt.type** indicates its type.

When you declare a sequence or choice of elements, you can specify an occurrence indicator for each child element.

Here is an example of a set of occurrence indicators:

```
<!ELEMENT elt.list (elt1, elt2?, elt3+, elt4*)>
```

In this example, the **elt1** element has no occurrence indicator. This means that **elt1** must appear within the **elt.list** element, once and once only.

The occurrence indicator of the **elt2** element is **?**. This means that **elt2** must appear within the **elt.list** element either once or not at all.

The occurrence indicator of the **elt3** element is +. This means that **elt3** must appear at least once within the **elt.list** element and can appear more than once.

The occurrence indicator of the **elt4** element is *. This means that **elt4** can appear within the **elt.list** element, once or more or not at all.

1. Text element

This is the most common element because it contains text.

Here is an example of a text element declaration:

```
<!ELEMENT elt (#PCDATA)>
```

PCDATA stands for Parsed Character DATA.

2. Sequence of elements

A sequence of elements is a set of elements that a defined element must contain. This defined element can contain only this set of elements. Commas separate these elements, which appear between brackets.

The elements in the sequence of elements are called **child elements**. The DTD must declare each of these elements in the same order as they appear in the sequence.

Here is an example of a sequence of elements declaration:

```
<!ELEMENT elt.list (elt1, elt2, elt3)>
```

Here is an example of correct usage:

```
<elt.list>
    <elt1></elt1>
    <elt2></elt2>
    <elt3></elt3>
</elt.list>
```

Here is an example of incorrect usage:

```
<elt.list>
    <elt1></elt1>
    <elt3></elt3>
</elt.list>
```

In the above example, **elt2** is missing. Here is another example of incorrect usage:

```
<elt.list>
    <elt2></elt2>
    <elt1></elt1>
    <elt3></elt3>
</elt.list>
```

In the above example, the elements do not appear in the correct order.

Important note: the Internet Explorer XML parser does not generate an error when elements do not appear in the correct order.

3. Choice elements

How you can use choice elements depends on the occurrence indicators for the elements. The DTD must always declare the child elements. The choice elements appear in a list separated by the "|" (Alt Gr 6) character.

If you do not associate an occurrence indicator with your choice elements, you can use only one of them.

Otherwise, the rules for using choice elements are similar to those for using a sequence of elements. The main difference is that you do not have to use all the choice elements.

Here is an example of choice elements without an occurrence indicator:

```
<!ELEMENT choice.elt (elt1 | elt2 | elt3)>
```

Here is an example of correct usage:

```
<choice.elt>
    <elt2></elt2>
</choice.elt>
```

Here is an example of incorrect usage:

```
<choice.elt>
    <elt2></elt2>
    <elt3></elt3>
</choice.elt>
```

The above example uses one element too many.

Here is an example of a choice elements declaration with occurrence indicators:

```
<!ELEMENT choice.elt (elt1*|elt2*|elt3*)>
```

Here is an example of correct usage:

```
<choice.elt>
   <elt2></elt2>
   <elt3></elt3>
</choice.elt>
```

Here is an example of incorrect usage:

```
<choice.elt>
   <elt3></elt3>
   <elt2></elt2>
</choice.elt>
```

In the above example, the elements do not appear in the correct order.

Important note: the Internet Explorer XML parser does not generate an error when elements do not appear in the correct order.

Here is an example of a choice elements declaration with an overall occurrence indicator:

```
<!ELEMENT choice.elt (elt1|elt2|elt3)*>
```

Here is an example of correct usage:

```
<choice.elt>
   <elt2></elt2>
   <elt3></elt3>
   <elt1></elt1>
</choice.elt>
```

Unlike element-by-element occurrence indicators, with an overall occurrence indicator your choice elements do not have to appear in the order in which you declare them.

4. Empty element

As its name suggests, an empty element has no content.

You must use the **EMPTY** keyword to declare this type of element.

```
<!ELEMENT empty.elt EMPTY>
```

HTML also provided empty elements. With HTML you can specify a line break (**
), a horizontal rule (<hr>**) and an image (**<img src='logo.png' ...>**), for example. These elements do not need closing tags.

In HTML DTDs, a closing tag must not appear after an empty element.

You can represent an empty element in XML, as you would indicate one in HTML. The only difference is that with XML, as you create the elements yourself, you must indicate whether a tag is empty or not: for this purpose, you can use the empty tag indicator ("/>").

Here is an example of using an empty element:

```
<empty.elt/>
```

As XML is compatible with SGML, you can also use a closing tag to close your empty element.

Here is an example of using an SGML compatible empty element:

```
<empty.elt></empty.elt>
```

This statement is equivalent to the previous one.

You can include attributes or formatting items in empty elements. These techniques can be very useful.

5. Any element

An **any** element is the opposite of an **empty** element: it can contain anything the DTD allows. **Any** elements can appear in any order.

You must use the **ANY** keyword to declare this type of element.

Here is an example of an **any** element declaration:

```
<!ELEMENT any.elt ANY>
```

6. Mixed content element

A mixed content element is a choice element list that can also contain text. You can include the text anywhere in the element. This text can be a CDATA section.

Here is an example of a mixed content element declaration:

```
<!ELEMENT hi (#PCDATA | target)*>
```

Here is an example of using a mixed content element:

```
<hi>
   Hello
   <target>World</target>
</hi>
```

C. Declaring attributes

In addition to declaring elements, the DTD allows you to declare attributes and apply them to your elements. Attributes provide additional information. You can declare all the attributes for the same element at the same time using a list of attributes. You must use the **ATTLIST** keyword for this type of declaration. Each attribute has a name, a type and a default value.

There are three types of attribute: character strings, predefined types (such as ID, IDREF, ENTITY, NMTOKEN or NOTATION) and enumerated values.

1. Default values

Each attribute can be required, implied (optional) or fixed.

In all four examples below, the "elt" element has the "attr" attribute.

Here is an example of an attribute declaration with a default value:

```
<!ATTLIST elt attr CDATA "value">
```

When you omit an attribute that you declared with a default value, the application processor adds the attribute with its default value and does not generate an error.

Here is an example of a required attribute declaration:

```
<!ATTLIST elt attr CDATA #REQUIRED>
```

Here is an example of an implied (optional) attribute declaration:

```
<!ATTLIST elt attr CDATA #IMPLIED>
```

Here is an example of a fixed attribute declaration:

```
<!ATTLIST elt attr CDATA #FIXED "value">
```

If you omit a required attribute from an element, the application processor will generate an error. If the value of a fixed attribute is different from the value you declared in the DTD, the application processor will also generate an error.

2. Character string types

In a document that does not have a DTD, XML treats all attributes as character strings. A character string can contain characters and internal parsed entities (see section D of this chapter: Declaring entities).

You must use the **CDATA** keyword to declare a character string.

Here is an example of a CDATA attribute declaration:

```
<!ATTLIST elt attr CDATA>
```

Here is an example of using a character string attribute:

```
<elt attr="Character string">
```

Here is an example of using a character string attribute, with an entity declaration:

```
<!ENTITY chars "characters">
<elt attr="String of &chars;">
```

3. ID type

This type defines a unique identifier. Consequently, no two ID attributes can have the same value in the same XML document.

📎 ID values must respect the XML naming rules, except for the fact that the first character of the ID value cannot be a colon (:).

Here is an example of an ID attribute declaration:

```
<!ATTLIST elt attr ID>
```

Here is an example of correct usage:

```
<elt attr="_123A">
```

Here is an example of incorrect usage (the value begins with a digit):

```
<elt attr="123A">
```

4. IDREF and IDREFS types

These types reference ID attributes. The values of such attributes must correspond to the values of ID attributes in the XML document. The only difference between these two types is the number of ID values they can contain. An IDREF attribute can contain only one ID value. On the other hand, an IDREFS attribute can contain several ID values, separated by spaces.

Here are examples of IDREF and IDREFS attribute declarations:

```
<!ATTLIST elt1 attr IDREF>
<!ATTLIST elt2 attr IDREFS>
```

Here are examples of using IDREF and IDREFS attributes:

```
<elt1 attr="_123A">
<elt2 attr="_123A AB32">
```

5. ENTITY and ENTITIES types

These types call internal or external entities that the DTD defines. The values of these attributes are the names of the entities they call (see section D of this chapter: Declaring entities). An ENTITY attribute can reference only one attribute. On the other hand, an ENTITIES attribute can contain the names of several attributes, separated by spaces.

Here are examples of ENTITY and ENTITIES attribute declarations:

```
<!ATTLIST elt1 attr ENTITY>
<!ATTLIST elt2 attr ENTITIES>
```

Here are examples of using ENTITY and ENTITIES attributes:

```
<elt1 attr="AP">
<elt2 attr="AP PB">
```

6. NMTOKEN and NMTOKENS types

The value of an NMTOKEN or an NMTOKENS attribute is a character string, containing characters such as letters, digits, periods, colons, dashes and underscores. The values of these attributes must correspond to objects declared in the DTD (such as elements or attributes). As with IDREF and ENTITY, an NMTOKEN attribute can contain only one value, whereas an NMTOKENS attribute can contain several values, separated by spaces.

The difference with respect to the character string type is that the values of the NMTOKEN types must respect the XML naming rules.

7. NOTATION type

Do not confuse notation type attributes with notation declarations (see section E of this chapter: Declaring notations).

The notation attribute uses a notation declaration.

Here is an example of a NOTATION attribute declaration:

```
<!ATTLIST img
   format NOTATION (BMP) #IMPLIED
>
```

This example declares a **format** attribute of the **img** element that refers to a **BMP** notation.

Here is an example of declaring a list of NOTATION attributes:

```
<!ATTLIST img
   format NOTATION (BMP | GIF | JPEG) "GIF"
>
```

This example declares a list of notations as the **format** attribute. This approach allows the format to take one of the three defined types. For this declaration to be valid, you must have declared all the notations in the list.

8. Enumerated value types

The enumerated value type defines a choice list of possible values for an attribute.

The attribute must have a known value, as it must take one of the list values. This allows a style sheet to work directly with this value.

Here is an example of declaring a list of enumerated value attributes:

```
<!ATTLIST img
   format ( BMP | GIF | JPEG ) "JPEG"
>
```

This example declares a **format** attribute of the **img** element. The value of this attribute can be BMP, GIF or JPEG (if you do not specify a value, "JPEG" will be used, by default).

D. Declaring entities

1. Definable entity

Entities can be either predefined or definable.

Entities can contain text or binary code.

Here are examples of definable entity declarations:

```
<!ENTITY hi "Hello World!">
<!ENTITY test SYSTEM "test.gif" NDATA GIF>
```

When the XML processor finds a call to an entity, it replaces it by its contents.

This example shows how you can declare and use a definable entity:

```
<?xml version="1.0" encoding="UTF-8"?>
<!DOCTYPE hi [
   <!ENTITY hi "Hello World!">
]>
<hi>
   &hi;
</hi>
```

Here is the result of this XML code in a browser:

This example associates an XML document with a DTD that contains the **hi** entity. The XML document calls the **hi** entity in its document element. The result in the browser shows how the XML processor replaces this call by its contents.

You can also reference an entity in another entity declaration.

Here is an example of this approach:

```
<!ENTITY target "World">
<!ENTITY hi "Hello &target;!">
```

2. Predefined entity

Predefined entities allow you to use those characters that the XML parser would otherwise interpret as system characters. For example, suppose you want to display the sentence "This is an <XML> document". If you enter this sentence directly, the XML parser will interpret the < and > characters.

In this case, you must use predefined entities.

Here is a summary of the predefined entities:

```
&       &amp; or &#38;#38;
'       &apos; or &#39;
>       &gt; or &#62;
<       &lt; or &#38;#60;
"       &quot; or &#34;
```

Using these predefined entities, you would write this sentence as follows:

```
This is an &lt;XML&gt; document
```

3. Parsed entity

Parsed entities contain text and can appear in the DTD or in the XML document. In all cases, the XML parser replaces calls to these entities with the corresponding text.

4. Non-parsed entity

Non-parsed entities generally refer to binary contents, such as an image, for example. Binary content is not parsed.

You can declare a non-parsed entity as you would declare a parsed entity, except that you must previously have declared the non-parsed entity format and the application that must process this format. For this purpose, you must use the **NOTATION** keyword (see section E of this chapter: Declaring notations).

Here is an example of a non-parsed entity declaration:

```
<!NOTATION GIF SYSTEM "iexplore.exe">
<!ENTITY test SYSTEM "test.gif" NDATA GIF>
```

This example defines a **test** entity that corresponds to the **test.gif** image. The **NDATA** parameter indicates that the file is not in XML format. Immediately afterwards, this statement specifies that this file has a GIF format.

The preceding **NOTATION** statement indicates that the **iexplore.exe** application will process all GIF formats.

The **SYSTEM** keyword indicates that the resource is a private one. You could replace this keyword by the **PUBLIC** keyword, to indicate that everyone can access this resource via a URI *(Uniform Resource Identifier)*.

Unlike parsed entities, you call a non-parsed entity directly by its name. You must assign the reference to the attribute of an empty ENTITY type element.

Here is an example of a non-parsed entity call:

```
<root.test root.attr='test'/>
```

The following example shows how you can declare and use a non-parsed entity:

```
<?xml version="1.0"?>
<!DOCTYPE root.test [
   <!NOTATION GIF SYSTEM "iexplore.exe">
   <!ENTITY test SYSTEM "test.gif" NDATA GIF>
   <!ELEMENT root.test EMPTY>
   <!ATTLIST root.test
       root.attr ENTITY #REQUIRED
   >
]>
<root.test root.attr='test'/>
```

5. Internal entity

Internal entities use resources that are either in the XML document or in the DTD. In each entity declaration you assign a value to a name. You use the name you declare to call the entity. When the XML processor finds a call to the entity in the document, it replaces it by the value in your declaration.

6. External entity

External entities allow you to segment a document into several separate documents.

Suppose you are writing a report or a book, for example. You can use external elements to split your book into chapters.

This example shows how you can declare and use an external entity:

```
<?xml version="1.0" encoding="UTF-8"?>
<!DOCTYPE book [
   <!ENTITY chapter1 SYSTEM "chap1.xml">
   <!ENTITY chapter2 SYSTEM "chap2.chap">
   <!ENTITY chapter3 SYSTEM "chap3.txt">
]>
<book>
   <intro>Add the files</intro>
   <chapter>&chapter1;</chapter>
   <chapter>&chapter2;</chapter>
   <chapter>&chapter3;</chapter>
</book>
```

This example declares three entities. Each entity calls a different file: an .XML file, a .chap file (containing raw text) and a .txt file. In the XML document, a separate "chapter" element calls each of these entities.

Each of these files contains the sentence "This is chapter x", with x being the chapter number.

Here is the result in Internet Explorer:

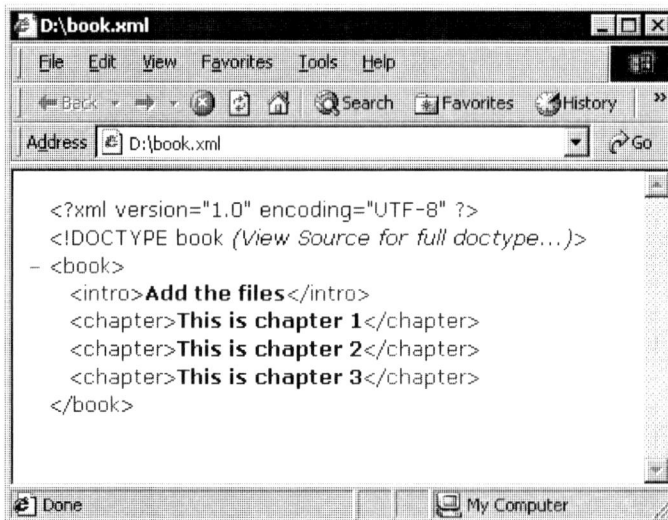

Implementing XML

The XML processor replaces each call by the contents of the corresponding file.

7. Summary

Here is a brief comparative definition of internal/external parsed/non-parsed entities:

Internal parsed entity   an internal entity with parsed text.

Internal non-parsed entity   an internal entity with non-parsed text.

External parsed entity   an entity that calls an external document containing parsed text.

External non-parsed entity   an entity that calls an external document containing binary code or non-parsed text.

E. Declaring notations

Here is the format of a notation declaration:

```
<!NOTATION format SYSTEM "application">
```

This declaration associates an application with an entity format that the XML processor would not otherwise have recognized. In general, you use notations with non-parsed entities (see section D of this chapter: Declaring entities).

> Notations come from SGML and are not used very much in XML: Xlink is often used instead (however, Internet Explorer does not support the Xlink specification, which has not yet reached the recommendation stage).

F. Valid document and well formed document

Thanks to its descriptive data, XML allows you to create structured documents that are easy to understand. Furthermore, XML provides two validation concepts for a document: valid document and well formed document.

1. Valid document

A valid XML document is linked to a DTD and respects all the construction rules that this DTD defines.

The XML processor looks in the DTD for a definition of each element, attribute and entity in the XML document. If the XML document finds an error, it notifies the application.

Valid documents are particularly useful when you use style sheets (XSL). As noted earlier in this chapter, you can reuse a DTD with other XML documents. Moreover, you can reuse any style sheet associated with the DTD. This is especially convenient, as style sheets often take a long time to set up.

2. Well formed document

A well formed XML document must simply comply with the XML syntax rules.

The XML syntax rules are much less strict than XML validity rules. XML syntax rules cover name assignment and element creation and nesting.

Well formed documents make it simpler to create XML code. Valid documents are much more restrictive.

However, each of these concepts offers an advantage. For example, as a well formed document does not require a DTD, it allows a smaller file size and requires less bandwidth in the case of Internet applications.

Chapter 4: Style sheets

As this book noted earlier, XML separates the data you use and the description of how you want to display this data. This feature allows you to structure your document first, then concentrate on its format and appearance.

XML offers several processes for this purpose, such as CSS *(Cascading Style Sheets)* and XSL *(eXtensible Stylesheet Language)*.

The CSS process comes from HTML. It helps you to format text at paragraph and character levels. CSS helps you to display element contents. However, it does not allow you to add anything or even use the element names. XSL is more comprehensive and dynamic than CSS. XSL allows you to use element names, to display element content and to use information from the XML document according to the conditions the XSL defines.

A. Formatting with CSS

CSS stands for Cascading Style Sheets.

CSS allows you to specify numerous properties, such as font color, numbered and non-numbered lists. However, the browsers do not support all of these properties.

Although CSS does not allow more sophisticated formatting, it is suitable for formatting an XML document that contains text.

You can declare a style sheet in three ways. Firstly, you can declare a style sheet in a CSS file. You can associate your CSS file with your (HTML, XML or XSL) document either via an HTML **<link>** element or via an XML processing instruction.

Secondly, you can include the CSS declarations in an HTML **<style>** tag. Finally, you can use in-line styling, with which you add to each element, a **style** attribute containing a style sheet.

With the first two methods, you must declare your style elements as follows:

```
elt {
    property_1:value;
    property_2:value;
}
```

Here is the format you must use for in-line styling:

```
<elt style="prop_1:value; prop_2:value;" >
```

with **elt** being the element to which you are assigning the properties.

> Important note: you use a colon (:) to assign a property and a semi-colon (;) to separate your assignments.

Example of an HTML document associated with a CSS style sheet

```
<!DOCTYPE HTML PUBLIC "-//W3C//DTD HTML 4.0 Transitional//EN">
<html>
 <head>
  <title>Test CSS</title>
  <link rel="stylesheet" type="text/css" href="csshtm.css">
 </head>
 <body>
  <H1>Style sheets</H1>
<!-- section containing a glossary term and formatting using
the glossary class -->
  <div class=glossary>
<!-- sub-section containing the term to be defined and
formatting using the to_be_defined class -->
                                                   .../...
```

```
.../...
   <span class=to_be_defined>CSS :</span><br>
<!-- sub-section containing the meaning and formatting using
the signification class -->
   <span class=signification>Cascading Style sheets</span><br>
<!-- sub-section containing the definition and using the
section's formatting by default -->
   <span>CSS format HTML and XML documents by setting display
   attributes (font, size, color, etc.).</span><br>
  </div>
 </body>
</html>
```

Here is the associated CSS style sheet:

```
H1
{
   FONT-FAMILY: verdana;
   FONT-SIZE: 18pt;
   PADDING-BOTTOM: 5pt;
   BACKGROUND-COLOR: lightgrey;
   TEXT-ALIGN: center;
   TEXT-DECORATION: underline;
}
.glossary
{
   FONT-SIZE: 12pt;
   FONT-FAMILY: verdana;
}
.to_be_defined
{
   FONT-SIZE: 15pt;
}
.signification
{
   FONT-WEIGHT: bolder;
   FONT-STYLE: italic;
}
```

Here is the result in a browser:

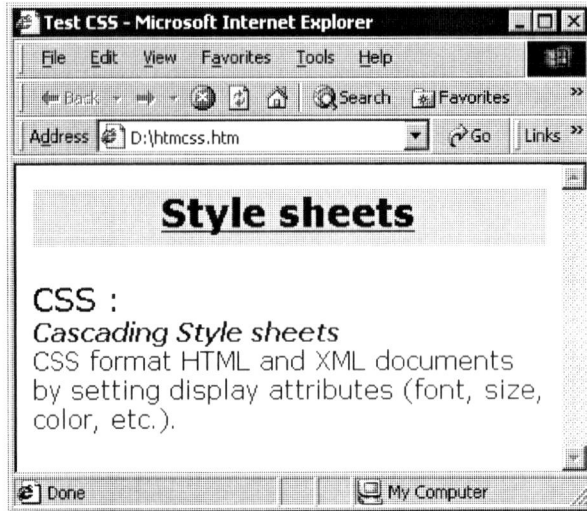

As the CSS source code above illustrates, with HTML you do not have to define all the elements. Element definitions can be inherited. The CSS defines the **glossary** class with two properties: **FONT-SIZE: 12pt** and **FONT-FAMILY: verdana** (12pt verdana font). This means that the default font for **DIV** elements of the **glossary** class is 12pt Verdana. This font will apply to each of these elements, as long as the element does not redefine the **FONT-SIZE** or the **FONT-FAMILY** properties.

To obtain the same result in XML, you need to make a certain number of changes to this code.

In HTML, you can specify a line break in a number of ways: by indicating the end of a **DIV** element, by using the **p** element or by using the **br** element, for example.

In XML and CSS, you specify a line break using the equivalent of the **DIV** element: the **DISPLAY:block** CSS property.

Example of an XML document associated with a CSS style sheet

```
<?xml version="1.0" encoding="ISO-8859-1"?>
<?xml-stylesheet type="text/css" href="xmlcss.css"?>
<page>
   <titleStyle sheets</title>
<!-- new glossary term to define -->
   <glossary>
<!-- term to define -->
      <to_be_defined>CSS :</to_be_defined>
<!-- meaning of the term -->
      <signification>Cascading Style Sheets </signification>
<!-- defining the term -->
      <definition>CSS format HTML and XML documents by setting
      display attributes (font, size, color, etc.).</definition>
   </glossary>
</page>
```

Here is the associated CSS style sheet:

```
page
{
   FONT-FAMILY: verdana;
   FONT-SIZE: 12pt;
}
glossary
{
}
title
{
   DISPLAY: block;
   FONT-SIZE: 18pt;
   PADDING-BOTTOM: 5pt;
   BACKGROUND-COLOR: lightgrey;
   TEXT-ALIGN: center;
   TEXT-DECORATION: underline;
   FONT-WEIGHT: bolder;
                                              .../...
```

Managing and formatting data

```
.../...
}
to_be_defined
{
   PADDING-TOP: 5pt;
   DISPLAY: block;
   FONT-SIZE: 15pt;
   PADDING-BOTTOM: 3pt;
}
signification
{
   DISPLAY: block;
   FONT-WEIGHT: bolder;
   FONT-STYLE: italic;
   PADDING-BOTTOM: 3pt;
}
definition
{
   DISPLAY: block;
   PADDING-BOTTOM: 3pt;
}
```

Here is the result in Internet Explorer 5:

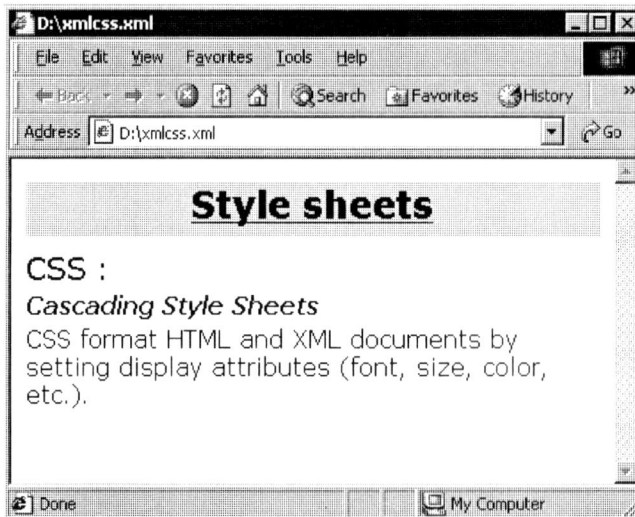

Implementing XML

Results are most often displayed with Internet Explorer 5, as the Netscape 6 and Opera 5 browsers generate only XML and not XSL.

Here is the above example displayed with these two browsers. Notice that they do not generate the CSS in the same way as Internet Explorer 5 does.

Here is the result in Netscape 6:

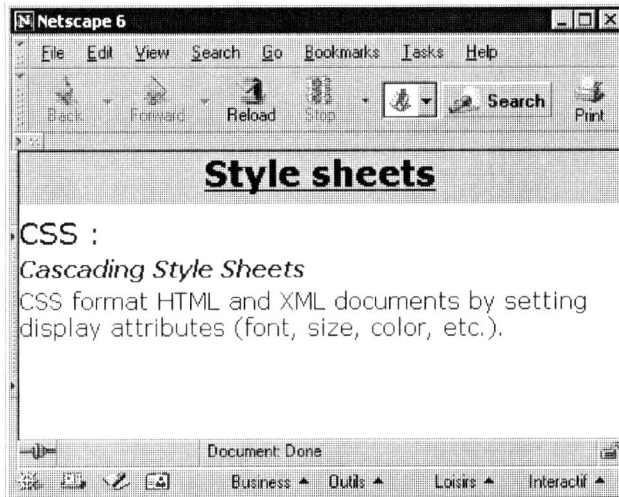

Here is the result in Opera 5:

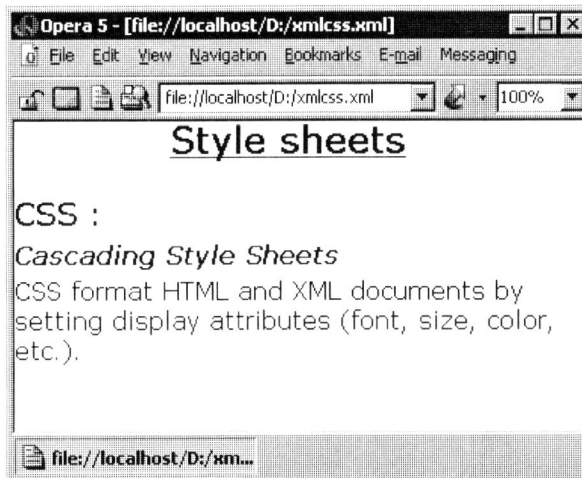

Notice that Opera 5 does not show the title background color. At the time of writing, Opera did not handle this property correctly.

The HTML code and the XML code produce the identical results, since the HTML code does not contain any elements that CSS cannot handle. On the other hand, you would not be able to use CSS to display a list (either numbered or not). Although CSS supports these features, currently available browsers do not handle them correctly.

One way of not being dependent on XML-specific elements is to use an HTML namespace.

In fact, this is the best way to use namespaces. They are commonly used in XSL files, which specify formatting and display parameters.

When you want to use only a CSS file, this approach allows you to add items such as tables and lists (either numbered or not).

Example of an XML document associated with a CSS style sheet and an HTML namespace

```
<?xml version="1.0" encoding="ISO-8859-1"?>
<?xml-stylesheet type="text/css" href="xmlcssns.css"?>
<page xmlns:html="htmluri">
<!-- title element of the HTML-specific namespace -->
   <html:title>XML test with CSS and NAMESPACE</html:title>
   <title>Style sheets</title>
<!-- br element of the HTML-specific namespace -->
 · <html:br/>
   <glossary>
       <to_be_defined>CSS :</to_be_defined>
<!-- br element of the HTML-specific namespace -->
       <html:br/>
       <signification>Cascading Style Sheets </signification>
       <html:br/>
                                                    .../....
```

```
.../...
        <definition> CSS format HTML and XML documents by setting
        display attributes (font, size, color, etc.).</definition>
        <html:br/>
!-- hr element of the HTML-specific namespace -->
        <html:hr/>
    </glossary>
</page>
```

Here is the associated CSS style sheet:

```
page
{
    FONT-FAMILY: verdana;
    FONT-SIZE: 12pt;
}
glossary
{
}
title
{
    DISPLAY: block;
    FONT-SIZE: 18pt;
    BACKGROUND-COLOR: lightgrey;
    TEXT-ALIGN: center;
    TEXT-DECORATION: underline;
    PADDING-BOTTOM: 5pt;
    FONT-WEIGHT: bolder;
}
to_be_defined
{
    FONT-SIZE: 15pt;
    PADDING-BOTTOM: 3pt;
}
signification
{
                                                        .../...
```

```
.../...
    FONT-WEIGHT: bolder;
    FONT-STYLE: italic;
    PADDING-BOTTOM: 3pt;
}
definition
{
    PADDING-BOTTOM: 3pt;
}
```

Here is the result in a browser:

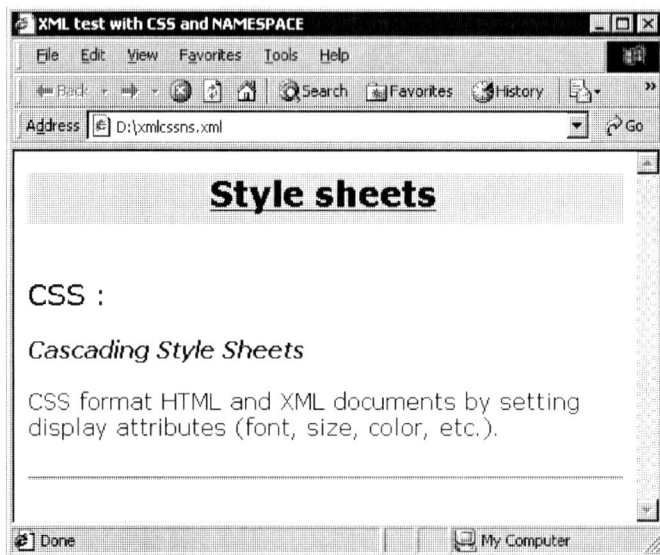

This example is very similar to the previous one, except that it declares a namespace in the opening tag of the **page** element (`<page xmlns:html="htmluri">`). The **xmlns** (XML namespace) attribute declares the name "html", as the generic URI "htmluri". This tells the browser that the html namespace concerns HTML elements.

Implementing XML

Once you have declared this namespace, you can use an html element by prefixing **html:** to its name. This example adds the title in the browser title bar via the **<html:title>** element. The **<html:br/>** line-break tag replaces the **DISPLAY:block** properties in the associated style sheet.

This technique declares an empty **br** element that the html namespace defines. This example also includes a horizontal rule: this is the empty **hr** element that the **<html:hr/>** tag defines.

Using namespaces in an XML document is incompatible with a document type declaration. This means that you cannot create a **valid** document: you can create only a **well formed** document. You cannot use DTDs with namespaces because the DTD must declare any tag you add. For example, this would lead to a double declaration of **<html:br>**, as the namespace already declares this element.

B. Formatting with XSL (XSLT)

1. Overview

XSL stands for eXtensible Style Language.

XSLT stands for eXtensible Style Language Transformation.

As its name suggests, XSL is a style sheet language. It is also a powerful element handler. It allows you to transform an XML source document by modifying its structure.

XSL works with templates. A template contains text (describing elements, attributes and text, for example) to replace a given element.

An XSL document is based on a **prolog** and an **<xsl:stylesheet>** element that can contain namespace declarations and the version number as attributes. XSL uses a generic namespace: uri.xsl. You can use this namespace for simple formatting operations.

The prolog contains the XML declaration, which indicates the version and the encoding used.

The XSL has a document element that contains all the templates, including template for the XML document element. This template corresponds to the element **<xsl:template match="/">**. The **match** attribute indicates that this template applies to the document element /. This document element contains several attributes, such as the version and namespace used.

Example of an XML document associated with a simple XSL document

```
<?xml version="1.0" encoding="ISO-8859-1"?>
<!-- associating with the XSL style sheet xmlxsl.xsl -->
<?xml-stylesheet type="text/xsl" href="xmlxsl.xsl"?>
<page>
   <title>Style sheets</title>
   <glossary>
      <to_be_defined>XSL:</to_be_defined>
      <signification>eXtensive Stylesheet
      Language</signification>
      <definition>XSL is a CSS-compatible style language.
      It also allows you to transform an XML document into
      another document.</definition>
   </glossary>
</page>
```

The only basic difference from the previous example is the style sheet call. The **type** attribute is **text/xsl** instead of **text/css** and the href attribute now refers to the XSL file.

Here is the associated XSL document:

```
<?xml version="1.0" encoding="UTF-8"?>
<!-- opening style sheet declaration -->
<xsl:stylesheet version="1.0" xmlns:xsl="uri:xsl">
<!-- template for the document element -->
   <xsl:template match="/">
      <html>
       <head>
          <title>XML test with XSL</title>
       </head>
       <body>
          <h1>
<!-- displaying the title element -->
            <xsl:value-of select="page/title"/>
          </h1>
<!-- displaying the to_be_defined element -->
            <xsl:value-of select="page/glossary/to_be_
            defined"/><br/>
<!-- displaying the signification element -->
            <xsl:value-of select="page/glossary/
            signification"/><br/>
<!-- displaying the definition element -->
            <xsl:value-of select="page/glossary/definition"/><br/>
       </body>
      </html>
   </xsl:template>
</xsl:stylesheet>
```

Here is the result in a browser:

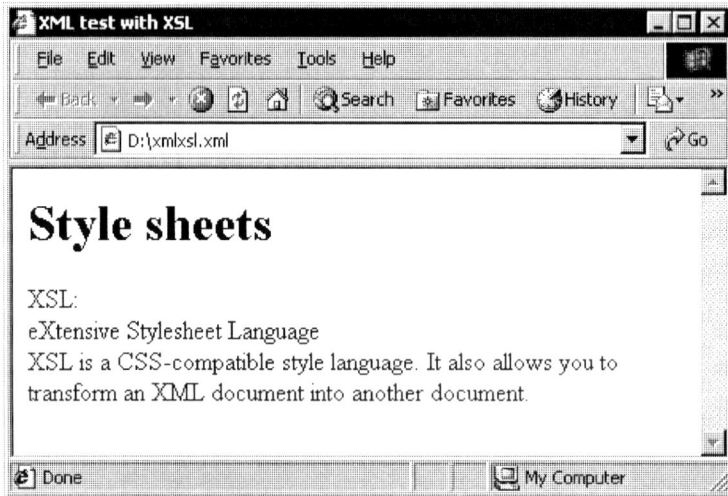

The source code in the example shows the minimum structure of an XSL document.

As the example must display the XML document in a Web browser, the template it applies to the document root is made up of HTML tags. These tags produce a basic HTML document.

The **<xsl:value-of select**="**element**"**/>** element displays the contents of the XML element. The **select** element contains a path that points to the element whose contents must be displayed. This path can be relative or absolute.

The above example uses simple formatting. You could format your document using HTML tags. However, it is preferable to use CSS.

Example of an XML document associated with a simple XSL document and a CSS file

```
<?xml version="1.0" encoding="ISO-8859-1" standalone="no"?>
<?xml-stylesheet type="text/xsl" href="xmlxslcs.xsl"?>
<page>
   <title>Style sheets</title>
   <glossary>
      <to_be_defined>XSL:</to_be_defined>
      <signification>eXtensive Stylesheet
      Language</signification>
      <definition>XSL is a CSS-compatible style language.
      It also allows you to transform an XML document into
      another  document.</definition>
   </glossary>
</page>
```

The XML document is the same as that in the previous example. The XSL document contains the link to the CSS document.

Here is the associated XSL document:

```
<?xml version="1.0" encoding="UTF-8"?>
<xsl:stylesheet version="1.0" xmlns:xsl="uri:xsl">
   <xsl:template match="/">
      <html>
        <head>
          <title>XML test with XSL and CSS</title>
<!-- linking the CSS style sheet xmlxsl.css with the XSL style
sheet -->
          <link rel="stylesheet" type="text/css"
          href="xmlxslcs.css"/>
        </head>
        <body>
         <h1>
            <xsl:value-of select="page/title"/>
                                              .../...
```

```
.../...
        </h1>
<!-- displaying the to_be_defined element -->
        <div class="to_be_defined"><xsl:value-of select=
        "page/glossary/to_be_defined"/></div>
<!-- displaying the signification element -->
        <div class="signification"><xsl:value-of select=
        "page/glossary/signification"/></div>
<!-- displaying the definition element -->
        <div class="definition"><xsl:value-of select=
        "page/glossary/definition"/></div>
      </body>
    </html>
  </xsl:template>
</xsl:stylesheet>
```

The style sheet links to the XSL document and also to an HTML document via the **link** element. This element has the same format as it would have with HTML, except that it is closed (as an empty element). The **div** tags specify the formatting.

Here is the associated CSS document:

```
body
{
   FONT-FAMILY: verdana;
   FONT-SIZE: 12pt;
}
H1
{
   FONT-SIZE: 18pt;
   PADDING-BOTTOM: 5pt;
   BACKGROUND-COLOR: lightgrey;
   TEXT-ALIGN: center;
   TEXT-DECORATION: underline;
   FONT-WEIGHT: bolder;
                                           .../...
```

K

.../...
}
.to_be_defined
{
   PADDING-TOP: 5pt;
   DISPLAY: block;
   FONT-SIZE: 15pt;
   PADDING-BOTTOM: 3pt;
}
.signification
{
   FONT-WEIGHT: bolder;
   FONT-STYLE: italic;
   PADDING-BOTTOM: 3pt;
}
.definition
{
   PADDING-BOTTOM: 3pt;
}
```

Here is the result in a browser:

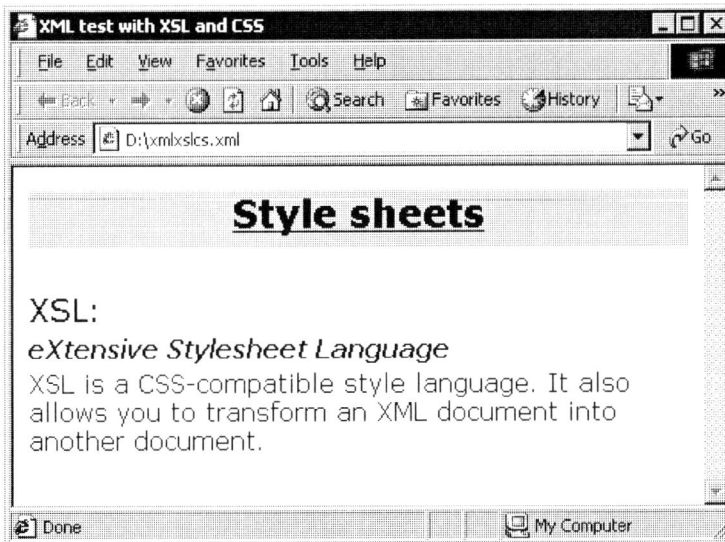

© Editions ENI - All rights reserved/

Managing and formatting data    77Managing and formatting data 77
```

2. XSLT elements

This section describes the different XSLT elements and gives examples of how you can use them.

> The examples in this section use the XSLT 1.0 namespace: "http://www.w3.org/1999/XSL/Transform". This namespace has reached the recommendation stage and offers the best compatibility with the Microsoft MSXML 3.0 parser.

<xsl:apply-imports>

This element allows you to apply a rule you have previously imported into your XSL document via the **<xsl:import>** element.

Associated element: **<xsl:import>**.

See the **<xsl:import>** example, below.

<xsl:apply-templates>

This element instructs the XSL processor to apply the appropriate template for each child element. In the absence of the **select** attribute, this element refers to the child elements of the current node.

You can use this element as follows:

```
<xsl:apply-templates
    select="node"
    mode="name"
>
```

select

defines the node whose child elements the XSL must process.

mode

specifies how XSL must process the elements: the XSL processor will apply the template that has a **mode** attribute with the same value.

See the **<xsl:template>** example, below.

<xsl:attribute>

This element defines an attribute and adds it to the transformed element.

You can use this element as follows:

```
<xsl:attribute name="name">value</xsl:attribute>
```

name

is the name of the attribute the XSL processor must add to the current context.

value

is the value the XSL processor must assign to the attribute.

Example:

Here is an XML document that calls an image:

```
<?xml version="1.0" encoding="UTF-8"?>
<?xml-stylesheet type="text/xsl" href="attribute.xsl"?>
<xsl.attribute>
     <image>test.gif</image>
</xsl.attribute>
```

Here is the associated XSL document:

```
<?xml version="1.0" encoding="UTF-8"?>
<xsl:stylesheet version="1.0"
xmlns:xsl="http://www.w3.org/1999/XSL/Transform">
<!-- image elements template -->
  <xsl:template match="image">
<!-- creating the HTML element img -->
     <img>
<!-- adding an src attribute pointing to the image -->
        <xsl:attribute name="src"><xsl:value-of
        select="."/></xsl:attribute>
<!-- adding an alt attribute describing the image -->
        <xsl:attribute name="alt">Testing attribute usage.
        Image: <xsl:value-of select="."/></xsl:attribute>
     </img>
  </xsl:template>
</xsl:stylesheet>
```

In this example, the XSL file defines an **<img>** element with two attributes: **src** and **alt**. To these attributes, it assigns the values "test.gif" and "Testing attribute usage. Image: text.gif", respectively.

Here is the result in a browser:

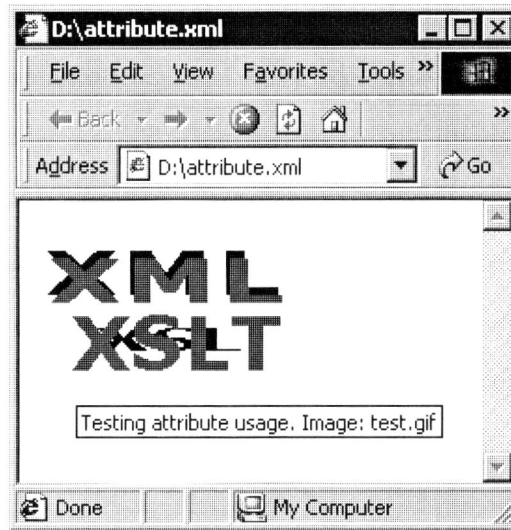

<xsl:attribute-set>

This element defines a set of attributes and gives it a name. This approach allows you to reuse this attribute set via the **use-attribute-sets** attribute, in the **<xsl:element>** element.

Associated element: **<xsl:element>**.

You can use this element as follows:

```
<xsl:attribute-set name="name">
```

name

is the name you give to the attribute set.

See the **<xsl:element>** example.

<xsl:call-template>

This element calls a template using its name.

You can use this element as follows:

```
<xsl:call-template name="template_name">
```

name

   is the name of the template you want to call.

<xsl:choose>

This element allows you to define a choose list and assign a different trans-formation to each choice. You can define each choice using an **<xsl:when>** element and you can specify default processing using an **<xsl:otherwise>** element.

Associated elements: **<xsl:when>** and **<xsl:otherwise>**

Example

This example applies a different background color according to the value of the **@type** attribute of the **spec** element.

```
<?xml version="1.0" encoding="ISO-8859-1"?>
<xsl:stylesheet version="1.0" xmlns:xsl="http://www.w3.org/
1999/XSL/Transform">
   <xsl:template match="/">
     <html>
        <body>
<!-- loop on each cd -->
         <xsl:for-each select="cd.list/cd">
            <xsl:apply-templates select="."/>
         </xsl:for-each>
        </body>
     </html>
   </xsl:template>
   <xsl:template match="cd">
     <xsl:choose>
<!-- the background color changes according to cd type -->
        <xsl:when test="spec/@type='Live'">
           <div style="background-color:lightblue">
              <xsl:apply-templates select="*"/>
           </div>
        </xsl:when>
        <xsl:when test="spec/@type='Soundtrack'">
           <div style="background-color:white">
              <xsl:apply-templates select="*"/>
           </div>
        </xsl:when>
<!-- default background color -->
        <xsl:otherwise>
           <div style="background-color:lightgrey">
              <xsl:apply-templates select="*"/>
           </div>
        </xsl:otherwise>
     </xsl:choose>
     <br/>
</xsl:template>
                                                    .../...
```

```
.../...
<xsl:template match="artist">
    <div class="artist">
        <xsl:value-of select="."/>
    </div>
</xsl:template>
<xsl:template match="title">
    <div class="title">
        - <xsl:value-of select="."/>
    </div>
  </xsl:template>
</xsl:stylesheet>
```

You can apply this XSL transformation to an XML document such as the following:

```
<?xml version="1.0" encoding="ISO-8859-1"?>
<?xml-stylesheet type="text/xsl" href="choose.xsl"?>
<cd.list>
  <cd>
    <artist>Keith Jarrett</artist>
    <title>Köln Concert</title>
    <spec type="Live"/>
  </cd>
  <cd>
    <artist>Keith Jarrett</artist>
    <title>Vienna Concert</title>
    <spec type="Live"/>
  </cd>
  <cd>
    <artist>Keith Jarrett</artist>
    <title>Dark Intervals</title>
    <spec/>
  </cd>
  <cd>
    <artist>Eric Clapton</artist>
    <title>Rush</title>
                                           .../...
```

```
.../..
    <spec type="Soundtrack"/>
  </cd>
  <cd>
    <artist>U2</artist>
    <title>Rock's Hottest Ticket</title>
    <spec type="Live" nb_cd="2"/>
  </cd>
</cd.list>
```

Here is the result in a browser:

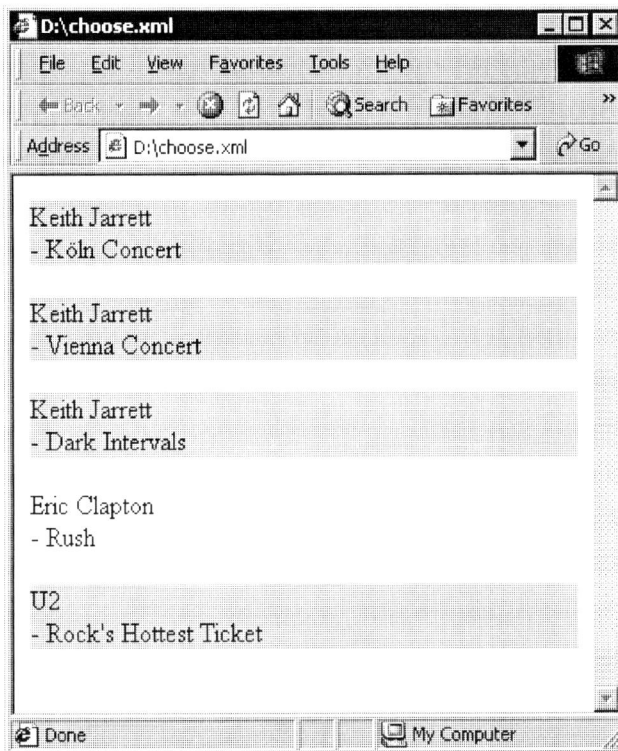

\<xsl:comment\>

This element allows you to add a comment to your transformation.

You can use this element as follows:

```
<xsl:comment>my comments</xsl:comment>
```

Here is the result of the transformation:

```
<!--my comments-->
```

\<xsl:copy\>

This element inserts a copy of the current node in the result of the XSLT transformation. By default, **\<xsl:copy\>** does not copy any of the element contents, not even its attributes. You can indicate what you want to copy via a template between the **\<xsl:copy\>** opening and closing tags.

Associated elements: **\<xsl:apply-templates\>** and **\<xsl:copy-of\>**.

You can use this element as follows:

```
<xsl:copy use-attribute-sets="att_set">
```

use-attribute-sets

   specifies the name of the attribute set you want to use for the copied elements.

Example

This example copies an element and adds a string of characters.

```
<?xml version="1.0" encoding="UTF-8"?>
<xsl:stylesheet version="1.0"
xmlns:xsl="http://www.w3.org/1999/XSL/Transform">
    <xsl:template match="*">
       <xsl:apply-templates select="*"/>
    </xsl:template>
    <xsl:template match="to_be_defined">
       <xsl:copy>
<!-- adding the character string -->
         Copy: <xsl:apply-templates select="text()"/>
       </xsl:copy>
    </xsl:template>
</xsl:stylesheet>
```

This example adds the string "Copy:".

It copies the **<to_be_defined>** element (alone) to the transformation along with its text, prefixed by the string **Copy:**.

You can apply this XSL transformation to an XML document such as the following:

```
<?xml version="1.0" encoding="ISO-8859-1" ?>
<?xml-stylesheet type="text/xsl" href="copy.xsl"?>
<page>
   <title>Style sheets</title>
   <glossary>
      <to_be_defined>XSL:</to_be_defined>
      <signification>eXtensive Stylesheet
      Language</signification>
      <definition>XSL is a CSS-compatible style language.
      It also allows you to transform an XML document into
      another document.</definition>
   </glossary>
</page>
```

Here is the result of the transformation:

```
<?xml version="1.0" encoding="ISO-8859-1"?>
<to_be_defined>Copy: XSL:</to_be_defined>
```

The transformation contains only the **<to_be_defined>** element.

<xsl:copy-of>

This element inserts a copy of the current node in the result of the XSLT transformation. Unlike **<xsl:copy>**, the **<xsl:copy-of>** element copies the whole subtree contents.

Associated element: **<xsl:copy>**.

You can use this element as follows:

```
<xsl:copy-of select="node">
```

select

   specifies the node you want to copy.

Example

This example copies an element.

```
<?xml version="1.0" encoding="UTF-8"?>
<xsl:stylesheet version="1.0"
xmlns:xsl="http://www.w3.org/1999/XSL/Transform">
   <xsl:template match="*">
     <xsl:apply-templates select="*"/>
   </xsl:template>
   <xsl:template match="to_be_defined">
                                              .../...
```

```
.../...
<!-- copy the entire current node -->
    <xsl:copy-of select="."/>
  </xsl:template>
</xsl:stylesheet>
```

This example copies the complete **<to_be_defined>** element into the transformation. You cannot specify additional content in the copy.

You can apply this XSL transformation to an XML document such as the
following:

```
<?xml version="1.0" encoding="ISO-8859-1" ?>
<?xml-stylesheet type="text/xsl" href="copy-of.xsl"?>
<page>
   <title>Style sheets</title>
   <glossary>
      <to_be_defined>XSL:</to_be_defined>
      <signification>eXtensive Stylesheet
      Language</signification>
      <definition>XSL is a CSS-compatible style language.
      It also allows you to transform an XML document into
      another document.</definition>
   </glossary>
</page>
```

Here is the result of the transformation:

```
<?xml version="1.0" encoding="ISO-8859-1"?>
<to_be_defined>XSL:</to_be_defined>
```

<xsl:decimal-format>

This element declares a decimal format that you can use as a pattern in the **format-number** function.

This element contains several attributes that have default values.

You can use this element as follows:

```
<xsl:decimal-format
   name="pattern_name"
   decimal-separator="char"
   grouping-separator="char"
   infinity="string"
   minus-sign="char"
   NaN="string"
   percent="char"
   per-mille="char"
   zero-digit="char"
   digit="char"
   pattern-separator="char"
/>
```

name

   specifies the format you want to call.

decimal-separator

   identifies the symbol you want to use as a decimal separator: the default value is a point (**.**).

grouping-separator

   identifies the symbol you want to use to separate the hundreds digit from the thousands digit and so forth: the default value is a comma (**,**).

infinity

specifies the string you want to use to represent infinity: the default value is the string **infinity**.

minus-sign

specifies the character you want to use to represent a negative number: the default value is the dash (-) character.

NaN

specifies the string you want to use to indicate that the value is not a number: the default value is the string **NaN**.

percent

specifies the string you want to use to represent a percentage: the default value is the **%** character.

per-mille

specifies the string you want to use to represent a per-mille (per thousand): the default value is the Unicode per-mille character **#x2030**.

zero-digit

specifies the character you want to use to indicate the digit zero: the default value is the digit **0**.

digit

specifies the character you want to use to indicate where a digit is required: the default value is the hash character (**#**).

pattern-separator

specifies the character you want to use to separate positive and negative sub-patterns: the default value is the semi-colon (**;**).

Managing and formatting data

Example

```
<?xml version="1.0" encoding="UTF-8"?>
<xsl:stylesheet version="1.0"
xmlns:xsl="http://www.w3.org/1999/XSL/Transform">
   <xsl:template match="/">
      <html>
        <body>
<!-- Creating a table -->
         <table>
            <col/><col style="text-align:right"/>
            <tr>
<!-- Defining the column headers -->
               <th>Item</th>
               <th style="text-align:center">Price</th>
            </tr>
            <xsl:for-each select="shop/item">
             <tr>
                <xsl:apply-templates/>
             </tr>
            </xsl:for-each>
         </table>
        </body>
      </html>
   </xsl:template>
<!-- Creating the digital display format -->
   <xsl:decimal-format
      grouping-separator=" "
      name="nbformat"/>
   <xsl:template match="*">
      <xsl:apply-templates select="item"/>
   </xsl:template>
   <xsl:template match="item">
      <td>
        <xsl:value-of select="."/>
      </td>
   </xsl:template>
                                              .../...
```

```
.../...
   <xsl:template match="Price">
      <td>
<!-- Applying the created format -->
         <xsl:value-of select="format-number(text(),
         '#  ###.00', 'nbformat')"/>
      </td>
   </xsl:template>
</xsl:stylesheet>
```

This example transforms the XML document into a table.

The table has two columns: one for the items and the other for the prices. The example pre-formats the prices using the **format-number** function. This function uses the following parameters: the string to convert, the display pattern for the number and a reference to the **<xsl:decimal-format>** element. This reference indicates the characters you can use in the display pattern.

You can apply this XSL transformation to an XML document such as the following:

```
<?xml version="1.0" encoding="ISO-8859-1" ?>
<?xml-stylesheet type="text/xsl" href="decimal-format.xsl"?>
<shop>
   <item>
      <item>Coffee table</item>
      <Price>945.9</Price>
   </item>
   <item>
      <item>Persian rug</item>
      <Price>1245</Price>
   </item>
   <item>
      <item>Chesterfield sofa</item>
      <Price>1950</Price>
   </item>
</shop>
```

Here is the result in a browser:

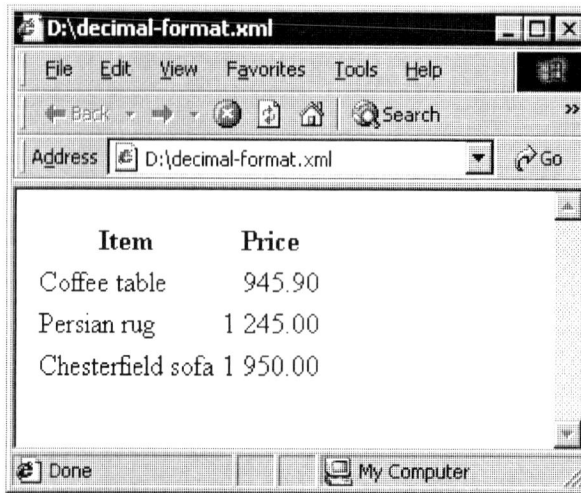

\<xsl:element\>

This element inserts a new element into the transformation. The **name** attribute specifies the name of the new element.

You can use this element as follows:

```
<xsl:element
    name="eltname"
    use-attribute-sets="att_set"
>
```

name

specifies the name of the element you want to create.

use-attribute-sets

specifies the name of the attribute set you want to use for your new element.

Example

This example inserts two elements and associates an attribute set with one of them.

```
<?xml version="1.0" encoding="UTF-8"?>
<xsl:stylesheet version="1.0"
xmlns:xsl="http://www.w3.org/1999/XSL/Transform">
<!-- creating an attribute set -->
   <xsl:attribute-set name="noborder">
<!-- adding a style attribute - value decoration:none -->
      <xsl:attribute name="style">{text-decoration:none}
      </xsl:attribute>
<!-- adding an href attribute whose value is that of the
address, child element that uses the attribute set -->
      <xsl:attribute name="href"><xsl:value-of select="address"/>
      </xsl:attribute>
   </xsl:attribute-set>
   <xsl:template match="/">
<!-- creating a document element called favorites -->
      <xsl:element name="favorites">
         <xsl:apply-templates/>
      </xsl:element>
   </xsl:template>
   <xsl:template match="*">
      <xsl:apply-templates select="*"/>
   </xsl:template>
   <xsl:template match="site">
<!-- creating for each site, a link to the site address using
the attribute set -->
      <xsl:element name="a" use-attribute-sets="noborder">
         <xsl:value-of select="text()"/>
      </xsl:element>
      <br/>
   </xsl:template>
</xsl:stylesheet>
```

This example creates the **<favorites>** element as a document element. It also associates a **noborder** attribute set with the **<a>** element it creates.

Managing and formatting data

This attribute set contains two attributes: the **style** attribute that removes the underline formatting from a link and the **href** attribute that contains the destination of the link.

You can apply this XSL transformation to an XML document, such as the following:

```
<?xml version="1.0" encoding="ISO-8859-1" ?>
<?xml-stylesheet type="text/xsl" href="element.xsl"?>
<favorites>
   <site>ENI Publishing
      <address>http://www.eni-publishing.com</address>
   </site>
   <site>ENI Consulting
      <address>http://www.eni-consulting.com</address>
   </site>
</favorites>
```

Here is the result of the transformation:

```
<?xml version="1.0" encoding="UTF-16"?>
<favorites>
   <a style="{text-decoration:none}"
      href="http://www.eni-publishing.com">ENI Publishing
   </a><br/>
   <a style="{text-decoration:none}"
      href="http://www.eni-consulting.com">ENI Consulting
   </a><br/>
</favorites>
```

Here is the result in a browser:

<xsl:fallback>

This element allows you to specify an alternative action for the XSL processor to take when it does not support the parent element. This element is useful when the version of your processor does not support an element you want to use.

XSLT version 1.1 introduced this element.

Example

This example calls an element the XSL processor does not support, without specifying an **<xsl:fallback>** element.

```
<?xml version="1.0" encoding="UTF-8"?>
<xsl:stylesheet version="1.1" xmlns:xsl="http://www.w3.org/
1999/XSL/Transform">
   <xsl:template match="image">
<!-- using an element that XSLT does not support -->
                                               .../...
```

```
.../...
      <xsl:show-image src="test.gif" alt="XML - XSLT
      illustration"/>
  </xsl:template>
</xsl:stylesheet>
```

This example uses a fictive element: **<xsl:show-image>**, which, of course, the current version of the browser does not support.

You can apply this XSL transformation to an XML document, such as the following:

```
<?xml version="1.0" encoding="UTF-8"?>
<?xml-stylesheet type="text/xsl" href="no-fallback.xsl"?>
<xsl.attribute>
   <image>test.gif</image>
</xsl.attribute>
```

Here is the result in a browser:

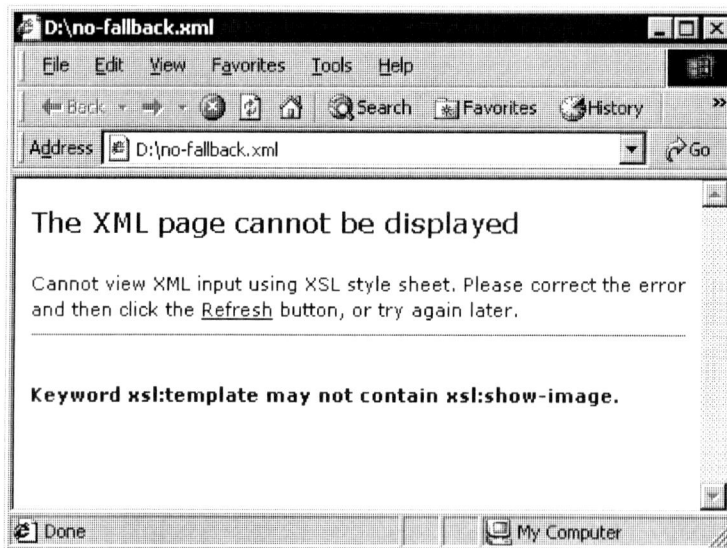

The **<xsl:fallback>** element allows you to solve this problem.

This example also calls an element that the XSL processor does not support, but this time, the example does specify an **<xsl:fallback>** element.

```xml
<?xml version="1.0" encoding="UTF-8"?>
<xsl:stylesheet version="1.1" xmlns:xsl="http://www.w3.org/
1999/XSL/Transform">
   <xsl:template match="image">
     <xsl:show-image src="test.gif" alt="Illustration XML -
     XSLT">
<!-- adding an alternative action for when the processor does
not support the previous element -->
       <xsl:fallback>
<!-- replacing the unsupported action with a standard HTML
display -->
         <img>
           <xsl:attribute name="src"><xsl:value-of select=
           "."/></xsl:attribute>
           <xsl:attribute name="alt">XML - XSLT illustration
           </xsl:attribute>
         </img>
       </xsl:fallback>
     </xsl:show-image>
   </xsl:template>
</xsl:stylesheet>
```

The above example uses the **<xsl:fallback>** element, to allow XLST processors that do not support the **<xsl:show-image>** element to carry out a similar transformation.

Here is the result in the browser when you apply this XSL transformation to an XML file with the same contents as the previous one:

This example replaces the **<xsl:show-image>** element with the contents of the **<xsl:fallback>** element without generating an error message.

<xsl:for-each>

This element creates a loop in which you can apply a certain number of transformations.

Associated elements: **<xsl:apply-templates>** and **<xsl:templates>**

You can use this element as follows:

```
<xsl:for-each select="node_set">
```

select

This attribute specifies the nodes that the loop must process.

Implementing XML

Example

```
<?xml version="1.0" encoding="ISO-8859-1"?>
<xsl:stylesheet version="1.0"
xmlns:xsl="http://www.w3.org/1999/XSL/Transform"
xmlns:fo="http://www.w3.org/1999/XSL/Format">
   <xsl:template match="/">
      <html>
        <head>
           <link rel="stylesheet" type="text/css"
           href="for-each.css"/>
           <title>CD list</title>
        </head>
        <body>
           <div class="pagetitle"><xsl:value-of select="cd_list
           /title.page"/></div>
           <br/>
<!-- Loop on all the CD list elements -->
           <xsl:for-each select="cd_list/cd">
              <xsl:apply-templates/>
           </xsl:for-each>
        </body>
      </html>
   </xsl:template>
   <xsl:template match="*">
   </xsl:template>
   <xsl:template match="artist">
      <div class="artist">
        <xsl:value-of select="."/>
      </div>
   </xsl:template>
   <xsl:template match="title">
      <div class="title">
        - <xsl:value-of select="."/>
      </div>
   </xsl:template>
</xsl:stylesheet>
```

In this example, the **<for-each>** element loops on the **<cd>** element, which is a child of the **<list.cd>** element. The processor applies the templates as long as it finds this element.

This example applies its templates to the **<artist>** and **<title>** elements. It formats the **<artist>** element using a CSS class and prefixes the contents of the **<title>** element with a dash.

Here is the CSS file:

```
BODY{
    font-family:verdana;
    font-size:"11pt";
}
.pagetitle{
    font-weight: bolder;
    color: #000080;
    font-size:"13pt";
}
.artist{
    font-weight: bolder;
    color: #000080;
}
.title{
}
```

You can apply this XSL transformation to an XML document, such as the following:

```
<?xml version="1.0" encoding="ISO-8859-1" ?>
<!DOCTYPE liste_cd SYSTEM "for-each.dtd">
<?xml-stylesheet type="text/xsl" href="for-each.xsl"?>
<cd_list>
    <title.page>CD list</title.page>
    <cd>
        <artist>Keith Jarrett</artist>
                                                    .../...
```

```
.../...
    <title>Vienna Concert</title>
    <spec type="Live"/>
  </cd>
  <cd>
    <artist>Keith Jarrett</artist>
    <title>Dark Intervals</title>
    <spec/>
  </cd>
  <cd>
    <artist>Eric Clapton</artist>
    <title>Rush</title>
    <spec type="Soundtrack"/>
  </cd>
  <cd>
    <artist>U2</artist>
    <title>Rock's Hottest Ticket</title>
    <spec type="Live" nb_cd="2"/>
  </cd>
</cd_list>
```

This XML document provides other information, such as the type and number of CDs. However, this example does not use this information.

This XML file uses the following DTD:

```
<?xml version="1.0" encoding="UTF-8"?>
<!ELEMENT cd_list (title.page, cd+)>
<!ELEMENT cd (artist, title, spec)>
<!ELEMENT title.page (#PCDATA)>
<!ELEMENT artist (#PCDATA)>
<!ELEMENT title (#PCDATA)>
<!ELEMENT spec (#PCDATA)>
<!ATTLIST spec
   type (Soundtrack | Live | Compilation) #IMPLIED
   nb_cd CDATA "1"
>
```

Managing and formatting data

Here is the result of the transformation:

```
<html>
<head>
<link rel="stylesheet" type="text/css" href="for-each.css">
<title>Liste de cds</title>
</head>
<body>
   <div class="pagetitle">CD list</div>
   <br>
   <div class="artist">Keith Jarrett</div>
   <div class="title">- Vienna Concert</div>
   <div class="artist">Keith Jarrett</div>
   <div class="title">- Dark Intervals</div>
   <div class="artist">Eric Clapton</div>
   <div class="title">- Rush</div>
   <div class="artist">U2</div>
   <div class="title">- Rock's Hottest Ticket</div>
</body>
</html>
```

Here is the result in a browser:

Implementing XML

<xsl:if>

This element allows you to fragment a template according to specific conditions.

You can test the presence of an element or an attribute. In addition, you can test to see if an element is the child of another element and you can test the values of elements and attributes.

You can use this element as follows:

```
<xsl:if test="condition">action</xsl:if>
```

test

Test takes the value of **1** or **0** according to the results of the **condition** ("true" or "false").

action

Action specifies the action that must be carried out (for example, to display text, to carry out a further test or to manage a string).

Here are some of the tests you can carry out:

```
<xsl:if test=".='text'">
```
tests whether or not the contents of the current element is equal to the string "text".

```
<xsl:if test="*">
```
tests the presence of an element in the current context.

```
<xsl:if test="elt">
```
tests the presence of the **elt** element in the current context.

```
<xsl:if test="elt='text'">
```
tests whether or not the string **text** contains the contents of the **elt** element from the current context.

```
<xsl:if test="@*">
```
tests the presence of an attribute in the current element.

```
<xsl:if test="@attr">
```
tests the presence of the **attr** attribute in the current element.

```
<xsl:if test="@attr='text'">
```
tests whether or not the string **text** contains the contents of the attr attribute from the current context.

```
<xsl:if test="elt[3]">
```
tests the presence of the third **elt** element in the current context.

```
<xsl:if test="/root/chap[3]/section[2]">
```
tests the presence of the second element **section** of the third element **chap**, child of **root**.

```
<xsl:if test="*/elt">
```
tests the presence of the **elt** element as grandchild of the current element.

```
<xsl:if test="../elt">
```
tests the presence of the **elt** element on the same level (sibling) as the current element.

```
<xsl:if test="/racine/*/elt">
```
tests the presence of the **elt** element as a grandchild of the document element.

```
<xsl:if test="//elt">
```

tests the presence of the **elt** element as a descendant of the document element.

```
<xsl:if test=".//elt">
```

tests the presence of the **elt** element as a descendant of the current element.

Example

This example tests the value of an attribute:

```
<?xml version="1.0" encoding="ISO-8859-1"?>
<xsl:stylesheet version="1.0"
xmlns:xsl="http://www.w3.org/1999/XSL/Transform">
   <xsl:template match="/">
      <xsl:value-of select="cd.list/title.page"/>
      <br/><br/>
      <xsl:for-each select="cd.list/cd">
         <xsl:apply-templates/>
      </xsl:for-each>
   </xsl:template>
   <xsl:template match="artist">
      <xsl:value-of select="text()"/>
      <br/>
<!-- Testing the value of the type attribute -->
<!-- If the value of type is Live, it displays Concert -->
      <xsl:if test="../spec[@type='Live']">Concert<br/>
      </xsl:if>
   </xsl:template>
   <xsl:template match="title">
         - <xsl:value-of select="text()"/>
      <br/><br/>
   </xsl:template>
</xsl:stylesheet>
```

This example tests the **type** attribute of the **spec** element. If its value is "Live", the example adds the **Concert** string along with a line break.

You can apply this XSL transformation to an XML document, such as the following:

```
<?xml version="1.0" encoding="ISO-8859-1"?>
<?xml-stylesheet type="text/xsl" href="if.xsl"?>
<cd.list>
   <title.page>CD list</title.page>
   <cd>
      <artist>Keith Jarrett</artist>
      <title>Vienna Concert</title>
      <spec type="Live"/>
   </cd>
   <cd>
      <artist>Keith Jarrett</artist>
      <title>Dark Intervals</title>
      <spec/>
   </cd>
   <cd>
      <artist>U2</artist>
      <title>Rock's Hottest Ticket</title>
      <spec type="Live" nb_cd="2"/>
   </cd>
</cd.list>
```

Here is the result in a browser:

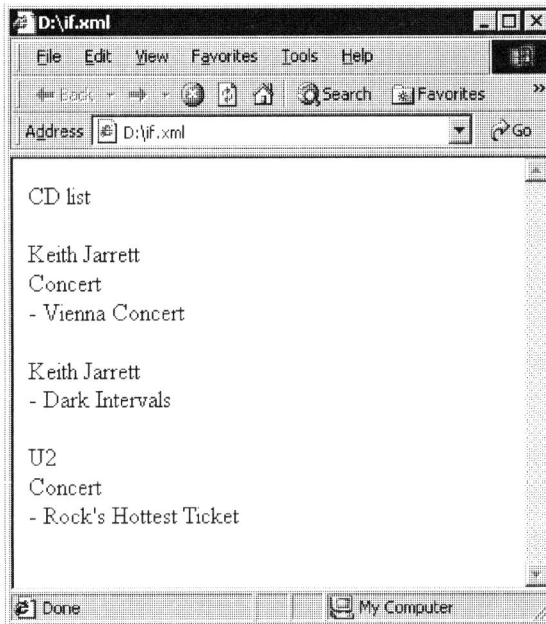

<xsl:import>

This element allows one style sheet to import another.

If both style sheets declare the same template and if the template the calling style sheet declares, uses the **<xsl:apply-import>** element, the two templates are combined. Otherwise, if this element is not used, the element the calling style sheet declares will be applied.

If a style sheet imports two other style sheets that contain the same template, the last template imported will be applied.

Associated element: **<xsl:apply-import>**.

◉ You must use this element before you define any templates. This element
must be a direct child of the document element.

Example

```
<?xml version="1.0" encoding="UTF-8"?>
<xsl:stylesheet version="1.0"
xmlns:xsl="http://www.w3.org/1999/XSL/Transform"
   <xsl:import href="import1.xsl"/>
   <xsl:import href="import2.xsl"/>
   <xsl:template match="*">
      <xsl:apply-templates/>
   </xsl:template>
   <xsl:template match="hello">
      <xsl:value-of select="."/> from Caller<br/>
   </xsl:template>
   <xsl:template match="hi">
      <div style="font:15pt"><xsl:apply-imports/></div>
      <br/>
   </xsl:template>
</xsl:stylesheet>
```

Here are the contents of the file import1.xsl:

```
<?xml version="1.0" encoding="UTF-8"?>
<xsl:stylesheet version="1.0"
xmlns:xsl="http://www.w3.org/1999/XSL/Transform">
   <xsl:template match="hello">
      <xsl:value-of select="."/> from Import 1<br/>
   </xsl:template>
   <xsl:template match="hi">
      <div style="color:lightblue"><xsl:value-of
      select="."/> from Import 1</div>
   </xsl:template>
</xsl:stylesheet>
```

Here are the contents of the file import2.xsl:

```
<?xml version="1.0" encoding="UTF-8"?>
<xsl:stylesheet version="1.0"
xmlns:xsl="http://www.w3.org/1999/XSL/Transform">
   <xsl:template match="hello">
      <xsl:value-of select="."/> from Import 2<br/>
   </xsl:template>
   <xsl:template match="hi">
      <div style="text-decoration:underline"><xsl:value-of
      select="."/> from Import 2</div>
   </xsl:template>
</xsl:stylesheet>
```

You can apply this XSL transformation to an XML file such as the following:

```
<?xml version="1.0" encoding="UTF-8"?>
<?xml-stylesheet type="text/xsl" href="apply-imports.xsl"?>
<apply>
   <hello>Hello</hello>
   <hi>Hi</hi>
</apply>
```

Here is the result in a browser:

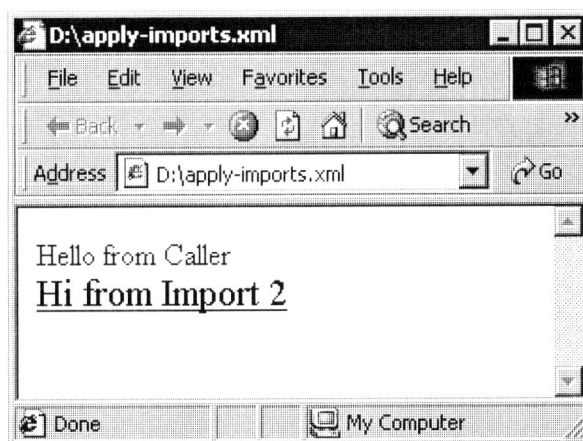

<xsl:include>

This element allows you to include an XSL style sheet in another XSL style sheet. This definition must appear on the level directly under the document element. Unlike the **<xsl:import>** element, the **<xsl:include>** element does not allow you to combine templates. If the calling document declares a template and the include document declares the same template, the template from the include file is applied.

You can use this element as follows:

```
<xsl:include href="URI">
```

href

This attribute is an URI that identifies the XSLT document to be included.

<xsl:key>

This element declares a named key. You can use it with the **key()** function, which returns a node set.

This element provides an easy way of selecting a specific node set.

You can use this element as follows:

```
<xsl:key>
   name="named_key"
   match="node"
   use="expression"
>
```

name

This attribute is the name of the key: the **key()** function uses this attribute to select the appropriate key.

match

This attribute indicates the node(s) the **key()** function must return.

use

This attribute specifies the expression that must be evaluated to test whether or not a node must be present in the node set. This expression is evaluated each time the **key()** function is called.

Example

This example uses a key with the **key()** function to select elements according to the value of an attribute.

```
<?xml version="1.0"?>
<xsl:stylesheet xmlns:xsl="http://www.w3.org/1999/XSL/
Transform" version="1.0">
<!-- defining the CD extraction key whose value of the type
attribute of the spec element corresponds to that passed as an
argument when called by key() -->
  <xsl:key name="type-cd" match="cd" use="spec/@type"/>
  <xsl:template match="cd.list">
    <cd.list.type.live>
<!-- using the key as a Live argument -->
      <xsl:apply-templates select="key('type-cd', 'Live')"/>
    </cd.list.type.live>
  </xsl:template>
  <xsl:template match="cd">
    <cd>
      <xsl:apply-templates/>
    </cd>
  </xsl:template>
  <xsl:template match="artist">
    <artist>
      <xsl:value-of select="."/>
                                                    .../...
```

```
.../...
      </artist>
   </xsl:template>
   <xsl:template match="title">
      <title>
         <xsl:value-of select="."/>
      </title>
   </xsl:template>
   <xsl:template match="spec">
      <nb_cd>
         <xsl:value-of select="@nb_cd"/>
         <xsl:if test="not(@nb_cd)">1</xsl:if>
      </nb_cd>
   </xsl:template>
</xsl:stylesheet>
```

This example declares a named key **type-cd**. It returns a set in which the **cd** elements are selected according to the value of the **type** attribute of the **spec** element of the **cd**.

The **key()** function uses this key, to select types with the **Live** value.

You can apply this XSL transformation to an XML document, such as the following:

```
<?xml version="1.0" encoding="ISO-8859-1" ?>
<?xml-stylesheet type="text/xsl" href="message.xsl"?>
<cd.list>
   <title.page>CD list</title.page>
   <cd>
      <artist>Keith Jarrett</artist>
      <title>Köln Concert</title>
      <spec type="Live"/>
   </cd>
   <cd>
      <artist>Eric Clapton</artist>
                                                    .../...
```

```
.../...
    <title>Rush</title>
    <spec type="Soundtrack"/>
  </cd>
  <cd>
    <artist>Keith Jarrett</artist>
    <title>Vienna Concert</title>
    <spec type="Live"/>
  </cd>
  <cd>
    <artist>Keith Jarrett</artist>
    <title>Dark Intervals</title>
    <spec/>
  </cd>
  <cd>
    <artist>U2</artist>
    <title>Rock's Hottest Ticket</title>
    <spec type="Live" nb_cd="2"/>
  </cd>
</cd.list>
```

Here is the result of the transformation:

```
<?xml version="1.0" encoding="ISO-8859-1"?>
<cd.list.type.live>
  <cd>
    <artist>Keith Jarrett</artist>
    <title>Köln Concert</title>
    <nb_cd>1</nb_cd>
  </cd>
  <cd>
    <artist>Keith Jarrett</artist>
    <title>Vienna Concert</title>
    <nb_cd>1</nb_cd>
  </cd>
  <cd>
                                                    .../...
```

```
.../...
    <artist>U2</artist>
    <title>Rock's Hottest Ticket</title>
    <nb_cd>2</nb_cd>
  </cd>
</cd.list.type.live>
```

<xsl:message>

This element allows you to send a message. The destinations to which you can send your message depend on the XSLT processor. You can send a message to a dialog box, a log file or the standard output.

The MSXML processor sends its messages to the browser.

You can use this element as follows:

```
<xsl:message terminate="yes"|"no">
```

terminate

This attribute can take the value **yes** or **no**. When **terminate** is equal to **yes**, the **XSLT** processor stops. For the MSXML processor, the default value of this attribute is **no**.

Example

This example displays a message if an attribute is absent.

```
<?xml version="1.0"?>
<xsl:stylesheet xmlns:xsl="http://www.w3.org/1999/XSL/
Transform" version="1.0">
   <xsl:output indent="yes" encoding="ISO-8859-1"/>
   <xsl:key name="cd-type" match="cd" use="spec/@type"/>
   <xsl:template match="cd.list">
                                                  .../...
```

Implementing XML

```
.../...
    <cd.list.type.live>
       <xsl:apply-templates select="key('cd-type', 'Live')"/>
    </cd.list.type.live>
  </xsl:template>
  <xsl:template match="spec">
    <nb_cd>
<!-- Testing for an nb_cd attribute -->
       <xsl:if test="not(@nb_cd)">
<!-- If this attribute is absent, display a message and stop
the XSLT processor -->
          <xsl:message terminate="yes">
            Number of CDs absent for the CD with the title:
            <xsl:value-of select="../title"/> by the
            artist: <xsl:value-of select="../artist"/>
          </xsl:message>
       </xsl:if>
       <xsl:value-of select="@nb_cd"/>
    </nb_cd>
  </xsl:template>
</xsl:stylesheet>
```

This example sends a message when the **nb_cd** attribute is absent from the **spec** element.

You can apply this XSL file to an XML document, such as that set out in the previous example.

Here is the result in a browser:

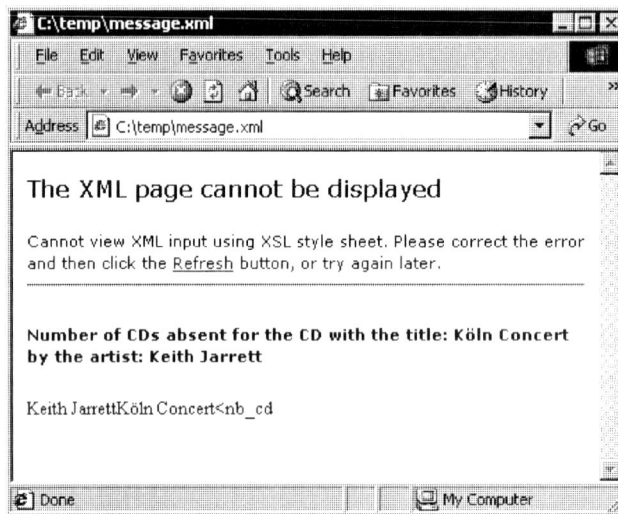

<xsl:namespace-alias>

This element allows you to give two different prefixes to the same name space.

As an XSL document can generate another XSL document, it is sometimes useful to dissociate the original namespace with the namespace you must generate.

You can use this element as follows:

```
<xsl:namespace-alias
    stylesheet-prefix="new"
    result-prefix="correspondence"
/>
```

stylesheet-prefix

This attribute indicates the name of the new prefix you want to associate with the **result-prefix** namespace.

Example

```
<xsl:stylesheet
xmlns:xsl="http://www.w3.org/1999/XSL/Transform"
xmlns:new="new" version="1.0">
<!-- Adding a second namespace -->
   <xsl:namespace-alias stylesheet-prefix="new"
   result-prefix="xsl"/>
   <xsl:param name="target" select="'cellular'"/>
   <xsl:template match="/">
<!-- Using the second namespace to transform this style sheet
into another, according to the value of the target parameter
-->
   <new:stylesheet>
      <xsl:choose>
         <xsl:when test="$target='cellular'">
<!-- Importing a target-specific style sheet into the style
sheet resulting from the transformation -->
            <new:import href="cellular.xsl"/>
            <new:template match="/">
               <div id='corps'>
                 <new:call-template name="display"/>
               </div>
            </new:template>
         </xsl:when>
         <xsl:when test="$target='assistant'">
            <new:import href="assistant.xsl"/>
            <new:template match="/">
               <div id='corps'>
                 <new:call-template name="display"/>
               </div>
            </new:template>
         </xsl:when>
         <xsl:otherwise>
           <new:import href="others.xsl"/>
           <new:template match="/">
               <div id='corps'>
                                                    .../...
```

```
.../...
                <new:call-template name="display"/>
            </div>
          </new:template>
        </xsl:otherwise>
      </xsl:choose>
    </new:stylesheet>
  </xsl:template>
</xsl:stylesheet>
```

This example defines a **new** namespace and associates a non-existent URL with it. Next, it associates this URL with the **xsl** namespace.

The XSL processor generates another XSL document whose contents depend on the target.

Here is the result of the transformation:

```
<?xml version="1.0" encoding="ISO-8859-1"?>
<xsl:stylesheet
xmlns:xsl="http://www.w3.org/1999/XSL/Transform">
   <xsl:import href="cellular.xsl" />
   <xsl:template match="/">
     <div id="corps">
        <xsl:call-template name="display" />
     </div>
   </xsl:template>
</xsl:stylesheet>
```

<xsl:number>

This element allows you to insert a formatted number that you can use as a counter.

You can use this element as follows:

```
<xsl:number
  level="single"|"multiple"|"any"
  count="node"
  from="node"
  value="expression"
  format="string"
  lang=nmtoken
  grouping-separator="char"
  grouping-size="number"
/>
```

level

This attribute indicates the levels you want to select for counting.

count

This attribute indicates the nodes that must be counted in the selected levels: if this attribute is not defined, the nodes with the same type as the current node are counted.

from

This attribute identifies the node from which counting must start.

value

This attribute specifies the expression corresponding to the counter value. If this attribute is not defined, the inserted number indicates the node position (**position()**).

format

This attribute specifies the number display format: this can be a digit or a character (a-z, A-Z) and it can include a separation character such as a dot (**.**) or a dash (**-**).

Here are some format examples: "1", "01", "a", "A", "i" and "I".

You can add separation characters to these formats.

lang

This attribute specifies the character set you want to use. By default, the system parameters decide this value.

grouping-separator

This attribute specifies the character you want to use to separate hundreds from thousands, for example. The **grouping-separator** and the **grouping-size** make up a set of attributes: if one of them is absent, the other is ignored.

grouping-size

This attribute specifies the number of characters in the group. The value of this attribute is often **3**. The **grouping-separator** and the **grouping-size** make up a set of attributes: if one of them is absent, the other is ignored.

Example

This example counts on two elements:

```
<?xml version="1.0" encoding="ISO-8859-1"?>
<xsl:stylesheet version="1.0"
xmlns:xsl="http://www.w3.org/1999/XSL/Transform">
   <xsl:template match="/">
      <html>
        <body>
           <xsl:value-of select="cd.list/title.page"/>
           <br/>
           <br/>
           <xsl:apply-templates select="//cd"/>
                                                   .../...
```

Implementing XML

```
.../...
        </body>
      </html>
   </xsl:template>
   <xsl:template match="cd">
<!-- Applying the counter -->
<!-- First level -->
      <xsl:number level="any" from="cd.list" count="type"
      format="A."/>
<!-- Second level -->
      <xsl:number level="any" from="type" count="cd"
      format="1. "/><br/>
      <xsl:apply-templates select="*"/>
   </xsl:template>
   <xsl:template match="artist">
      <xsl:value-of select="."/>
      <br/>
   </xsl:template>
   <xsl:template match="title">
       - <xsl:value-of select="."/>
      <br/><br/>
   </xsl:template>
</xsl:stylesheet>
```

First, this example counts the **type** elements in the document element then it counts the **cd** elements in the **type** elements. The count is indicated in an **A.1** type format:

A corresponds to the index of the **type** element in the **cd.list** element and **1** corresponds to the **cd** number in the **type** element.

You can apply this XSL transformation to an XML document, such as the following:

```
<?xml version="1.0" encoding="ISO-8859-1"?>
<?xml-stylesheet type="text/xsl" href="number.xsl"?>
<cd.list>
   <title.page>CD list</title.page>
   <type nom="Live">
      <cd>
         <artist>Keith Jarrett</artist>
         <title>Vienna Concert</title>
         <specif type="Live"/>
      </cd>
      <cd>
         <artist>U2</artist>
         <title>Rock's Hottest Ticket</title>
         <specif type="Live" nb_cd="2"/>
      </cd>
   </type>
   <type nom="Soundtrack">
      <cd>
         <artist>Eric Clapton</artist>
         <title>Rush</title>
         <specif type="Soundtrack"/>
      </cd>
   </type>
   <type nom="Studio">
      <cd>
         <artist>Keith Jarrett</artist>
         <title>Dark Intervals</title>
         <specif/>
      </cd>
   </type>
</cd.list>
```

Here is the result in a browser:

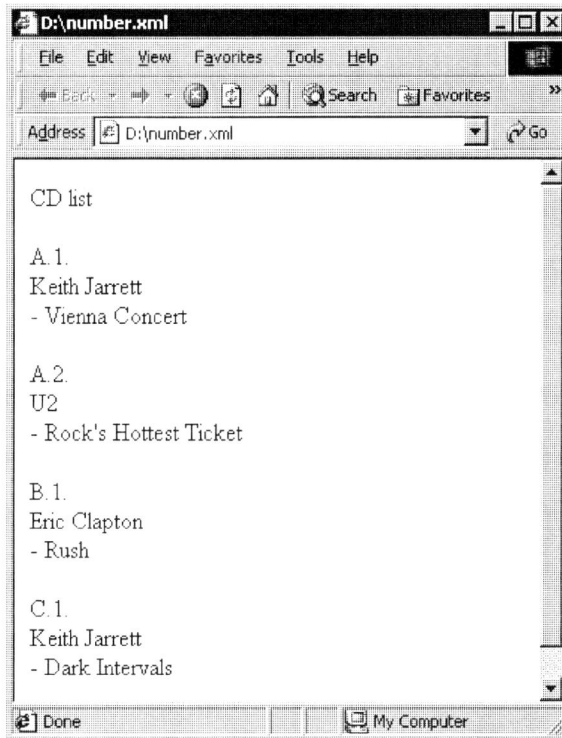

<xsl:otherwise>

This element provides a default action for the **<xsl:choose>** element.

Associated elements **<xsl:choose>** and **<xsl:when>**

See the **<xsl:choose>** example, above.

This element allows you to specify the format of the style sheet output.

You can use this element as follows:

```
<xsl:output
  method="xml"|"html"|"text"
  version="nmtoken"
  encoding="string"
  omit-xml-declaration="yes"|"no"
  standalone="yes"|"no"
  doctype-public="string"
  doctype-system="string"
  cdata-section-elements=elt
  indent="yes"|"no"
  media-type="string"
/>
```

method

This attribute specifies the transformation method: if this attribute is equal to **text**, no formatting will be applied.

version

This attribute indicates the output method version (xml 1.0 or html 4.0, for example).

encoding

This attribute indicates the character set version to be used for the output: this attribute allows you to display characters that do not belong to your current character set.

omit-xml-declaration

This attribute indicates whether or not the XSLT processor must add an XML declaration: if this attribute is equal to **yes**, the XSLT processor will not add an XML declaration.

Implementing XML

standalone

This attribute indicates whether or not the XSLT processor must create an output tree with a document type declaration.

doctype-public

This attribute specifies the public identifier the DTD associated with the transformation must use.

doctype-system

This attribute specifies the system identifier the DTD associated with the transformation must use.

cdata-section-elements

This attribute indicates the elements whose contents must be processed during the transformation via a CDATA section.

indent

This attribute presents the transformation in the form of a tree, when this attribute is equal to **yes**.

media-type

This attribute specifies the MIME type of the resulting transformation data.

<xsl:param>

This element allows you to declare a parameter you can use with the **<xsl:stylesheet>** and **<xsl:template>** elements.

Associated elements: **<xsl:with-param>**

You can use this element as follows:

```
<xsl:param
   name="param_name"
   select="value"
>text</xsl:param>
```

name

> This attribute contains the name of the parameter.

select

> This attribute contains an expression. The parameter value is the result of this expression. If this attribute is defined, the **<xsl:param>** must be an empty element.

text

> This attribute contains the value of the parameter, when the **select** attribute is not defined.

> See the **<xsl:with-param>** example below.

<xsl:preserve-space>

This element allows you to define elements in which whitespace nodes must be preserved.

This element is useful when the **<xsl:strip-space>** element has been used.

Associated elements: **<xsl:strip-space>**

You can use this element as follows:

```
<xsl:preserve-space elements="elt1 elt2"/>
```

elements

This attribute specifies the list of elements in which whitespace must be preserved.

By default, whitespace is preserved in all elements.

<xsl:processing-instruction>

This element allows you to insert a processing instruction in the transformation tree.

You can use this element as follows:

```
<xsl:processing-instruction name="pi_name">text</xsl:processing-
instruction>
```

name

This attribute specifies the processing instruction.

text

This attribute contains the contents of the processing instruction.

<xsl:sort>

This element allows you to sort a set of nodes. You can include this element either in an **<xsl:for-each>** element or in an **<xsl:apply-templates>** element.

This is an empty element. You can use it several times to carry out a sort with several conditions.

Each call to this element sorts on a specific field in a predefined order.

You can use this element as follows:

```
<xsl:sort
   select="node"
   data-type="text"|"number"|elt
   order="ascending"|"descending"
   lang=nmtoken
   case-order="upper-first"|"lower-first"
/>
```

select

> This attribute specifies a node as a sort key.

data-type

> This attribute indicates the type of data to be sorted. If you specify a **number** data-type, the data is converted before being sorted.

order

> This attribute specifies the sort order. This can be **ascending** or **descending**.

lang

> This attribute specifies the character set used for the sort. By default, it is determined according to system parameters.

case-order

> This attribute indicates whether upper-case letters must sort before lower-case letters, or vice-versa.

Example

This example sorts elements in ascending order.

```
<?xml version="1.0" encoding="ISO-8859-1"?>
<xsl:stylesheet version="1.0"
xmlns:xsl="http://www.w3.org/1999/XSL/Transform">
   <xsl:template match="/">
      <xsl:value-of select="cd_list/title.page"/>
      <br/>
      <br/>
<!-- looping on each CD in the list -->
      <xsl:for-each select="cd_list/cd">
<!-- sorting on titles in ascending order -->
         <xsl:sort order="ascending" select="title"/>
         <xsl:apply-templates/>
      </xsl:for-each>
   </xsl:template>
   <xsl:template match="artist">
      <xsl:value-of select="."/>
      <br/>
   </xsl:template>
   <xsl:template match="title">
       - <xsl:value-of select="."/>
      <br/>
      <br/>
   </xsl:template>
</xsl:stylesheet>
```

This example sorts the CD list in ascending order according to the **title**.

You can apply this to an XML document, such as the following:

```
<?xml version="1.0" encoding="ISO-8859-1" ?>
<?xml-stylesheet type="text/xsl" href="sort.xsl"?>
<cd_list>
   <title.page>CD list</title.page>
   <cd>
      <artist>Keith Jarrett</artist>
      <title>Vienna Concert</title>
      <specif type="Live"/>
   </cd>
   <cd>
      <artist>Keith Jarrett</artist>
      <title>Dark Intervals</title>
      <specif/>
   </cd>
   <cd>
      <artist>Eric Clapton</artist>
      <title>Rush</title>
      <specif type="Soundtrack"/>
   </cd>
   <cd>
      <artist>U2</artist>
      <title>Rock's Hottest Ticket</title>
      <specif type="Live" nb_cd="2"/>
   </cd>
</cd_list>
```

Here is the result in a browser:

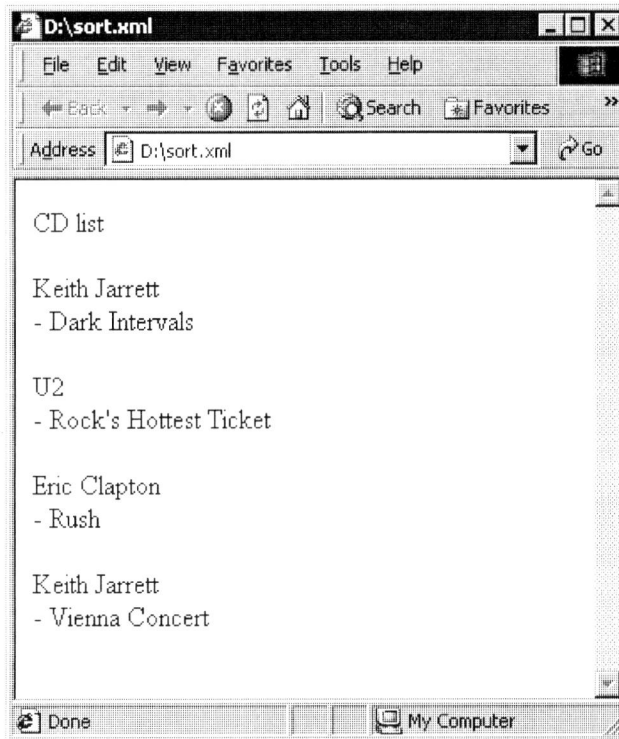

<xsl:strip-space>

This element allows you to define elements in which whitespace nodes must not be preserved. It indicates the elements in the source document whose whitespace content must be stripped.

Associated element: **<xsl:preserve-space>**

You can use this element as follows:

```
<xsl:strip-space elements="elt1 elt2"/>
```

elements

> This attribute specifies the list of elements whose whitespace content must be stripped.

<xsl:stylesheet>

This is the document element of the XSL style sheet. It contains all the other formatting elements.

You can use this element as follows:

```
<xsl:stylesheet
   id="id"
   version="number"
   xmlns:pre="URI"
>
```

id

> This attribute specifies a unique style sheet identifier.

version

> This attribute indicates the version of the XSLT style sheet. At the time of writing, this version could be **1.0** or **1.1**.

xmlns:pre

> This attribute defines the namespace. **pre** indicates the prefix that the style sheet must use to refer to the namespace URI.

<xsl:template>

This element defines a template that must be applied to a node and to a specific context.

You can use this element as follows:

```
<xsl:template
    name="template_name"
    match="expression"
    mode="template_mode"
>
```

name

This attribute indicates the name of the template. It refers to the **name** attribute of the **<xsl:call-template>** element.

match

This attribute contains an expression that specifies the nodes to which the template must be applied. This expression contains a match pattern defining an attribute set. For example, it can test the existence of an attribute and include the | character to indicate that the template must apply to one element or another.

mode

This attribute allows an element to have several templates, each generating a different output. The **<xsl:apply-template>** element allows you to define the template that must be applied, in addition to the mode that must be applied.

Example

This example applies two templates to an element.

```
<?xml version="1.0" encoding="UTF-8"?>
<xsl:stylesheet version="1.0"
xmlns:xsl="http://www.w3.org/1999/XSL/Transform">
   <xsl:template match="/">
      <html>
         <head>
            <title>Templates</title>
         </head>
         <body>
            <h1>
                <xsl:value-of select="page/title"/>
            </h1>
            <xsl:for-each select="page/glossary">
                <xsl:apply-templates select="."/>
            </xsl:for-each>
         </body>
      </html>
   </xsl:template>
   <xsl:template match="glossary">
      <xsl:if test="not(to_be_defined/@web)">
         <xsl:apply-templates select="to_be_defined"/>
      </xsl:if>
      <xsl:if test="to_be_defined/@web">
<!-- if the web attribute of the to-be-defined element exists,
apply the to-be-defined template in link mode -->
         <xsl:apply-templates select="to_be_defined"
         mode="link"/>
      </xsl:if>
      <xsl:apply-templates select="signification"/>
      <xsl:apply-templates select="definition"/>
   </xsl:template>
   <xsl:template match="to_be_defined" mode="link">
      <a href="http://{@web}">
<!-- if the web attribute of the to-be-defined element exists,
apply the to-be-defined template in link mode -->
         <xsl:value-of select="."/>
      </a>
                                          .../....
```

Implementing XML

```
.../...
      <br/>
   </xsl:template>
   <xsl:template match="to_be_defined">
      <xsl:value-of select="."/>
      <br/>
   </xsl:template>
   <xsl:template match="signification">
      <xsl:value-of select="."/>
      <br/>
   </xsl:template>
   <xsl:template match="definition">
      <xsl:value-of select="."/>
      <br/>
      <br/>
   </xsl:template>
</xsl:stylesheet>
```

This example defines several templates, including two templates for the **to_be_defined** element. One of these templates contains a **link** mode. The default template displays only the text of the **to_be_defined** element. The other of these templates transforms the text to a web site link, provided that the **web** attribute exists.

You can apply this XSL transformation to an XML document, such as the following:

```
<?xml version="1.0" encoding="UTF-8" standalone="no"?>
<?xml-stylesheet type="text/xsl" href="apply-templates.xsl"?>
<page>
   <title>XML et Style sheets</title>
   <glossary>
      <to_be_defined>CSS:</to_be_defined>
      <signification>Cascading Style Sheets</signification>
      <definition> CSS format HTML and XML documents by settin
      display attributes (font, size, color, etc.).</definition>
   </glossary>
                                                        .../...
```

```
.../...
   <glossary>
     <to_be_defined>XSL:</to_be_defined>
     <signification>eXtensive Stylesheet Language
     </signification>
     <definition>XSL is a CSS-compatible style language.
     It also allows you to transform an XML document into
     another document.</definition>
   </glossary>
   <glossary>
     <to_be_defined web="www.xmlfr.org">XML :</to_be_defined>
     <signification>eXtensible Markup Language </signification>
     <definition>XML is an extensible tagging language (you
     can create the tags you need for your application). The
     XML specification separates the data from the presentation
     of the data (which XSL supports).</definition>
   </glossary>
</page>
```

Here is the result in a browser:

<xsl:text>

This element generates text in the output tree. Placing several **<xsl:text>** elements next to each other groups the generated texts together.

You can use this element as follows:

```
<xsl:text
   disable-output-escaping="yes"|"no"
>text</xsl:text>
```

text

> This attribute contains the text to be added in the transformation.

disable-output-escaping

> This attribute indicates how special characters must be interpreted. If this attribute is set to **yes**, the sequence **&lt**, for example, will transform to the < sign, which can cause problems. If this attribute is set to **no**, the sequence **&lt**, for example, will be represented as it is in the transformation. In both cases, the browser will display the < sign.

<xsl:transform>

<xsl:transform> is a synonym for **<xsl:stylesheet>**.

Associated elements: **<xsl:stylesheet>**.

<xsl:value-of>

This element specifies an expression to insert the value of a node in the transformation.

This expression can indicate an element, an attribute or any other node that contains a value.

You can use this element as follows:

```
<xsl:value-of
   select="expression"
   disable-output-escaping="yes"|"no"
/>
```

select

The contents of this attribute are evaluated and the resulting value is inserted in the transformation.

disable-output-escaping

This attribute indicates how special characters must be interpreted. If this attribute is set to **yes**, the sequence **&lt**, for example, will transform to the < sign, which can cause problems. If this attribute is set to **no**, the sequence **&lt**, for example, will be represented as it is in the transformation. In both cases, the browser will display the < sign.

Most of the examples in this chapter use this element.

<xsl:variable>

This element allows you to assign a value to a variable. You can use this variable throughout your XSL document.

You can use this element as follows:

```
<xsl:value-of
   name="variable_name"
   select="expression"
>value</xsl:value-of>
```

Implementing XML

name

This attribute identifies the variable concerned.

select

This attribute specifies an expression that corresponds to the value of the variable. When this attribute is specified, the element must be empty.

value

If the **select** attribute is not defined, this attribute contains the value of the variable.

Example

This example declares and uses a variable to calculate a sale price from a normal retail price.

```
<?xml version="1.0" encoding="UTF-8"?>
<xsl:stylesheet version="1.0"
xmlns:xsl="http://www.w3.org/1999/XSL/Transform">
   <xsl:variable name="np2sp">0.80</xsl:variable>
   <xsl:template match="/">
      <html>
        <body>
<!-- Creating a table -->
          <table>
            <col/>
            <col width="100" style="text-align:right"/>
            <col style="text-align:right" width="100"/>
            <tr>
               <th>Item</th>
               <th style="text-align:right">Normal Price</th>
               <th style="text-align:right">Sale Price</th>
            </tr>
            <xsl:for-each select="shop/item">
                                                 .../...
```

```
.../...
                  <tr>
                     <xsl:apply-templates/>
                  </tr>
               </xsl:for-each>
            </table>
          </body>
        </html>
    </xsl:template>
    <xsl:decimal-format grouping-separator=" " name="nbformat"/>
    <xsl:template match="*">
       <xsl:apply-templates select="item"/>
    </xsl:template>
    <xsl:template match="item">
      <td>
         <xsl:value-of select="."/>
      </td>
    </xsl:template>
    <xsl:template match="Price">
      <td>
         <xsl:value-of select="format-number(text(),
         '#  ###.00', 'nbformat')"/>
      </td>
  <!-- Displaying value multiplied by the np2sp variable -->
      <td>
         <xsl:value-of select="format-number(number()*$np2sp,
         '# ###.00', 'nbformat')"/>
      </td>
    </xsl:template>
</xsl:stylesheet>
```

This example declares the **np2sp** variable. It uses this variable to calculate a sale price from a normal retail price. The template that processes the **Price** element uses this variable. The **number()** function extracts the contents of **Price** as a number and multiplies this value by that of the **np2sp** variable.

You can apply this XSL transformation to an XML file such as the following:

```
<?xml version="1.0" encoding="ISO-8859-1" ?>
<?xml-stylesheet type="text/xsl" href="variable.xsl"?>
<shop>
   <item>
      <item>Coffee table</item>
      <Price>945.9</Price>
   </item>
   <item>
      <item>Persian rug</item>
      <Price>1245</Price>
   </item>
   <item>
      <item>Chesterfield sofa</item>
      <Price>1950</Price>
   </item>
</shop>
```

Here is the result in a browser:

<xsl:when>

This element provides a conditional test that you can use within the **<xsl:choose>** element.

Associated elements: **<xsl:choose>** and **<xsl:otherwise>**.

You can use this element as follows:

```
<xsl:when
   test="expression"
>action</xsl:when>
```

test

This attribute contains the expression to be evaluated. This evaluation produces a Boolean value. The action will run if this Boolean value is "true".

See the **<xsl:choose>** example above.

<xsl:with-param>

This element allows you to pass a parameter to a template that you call using the **<xsl:xall-template>** element.

Associated element: **<xsl:param>**.

You can use this element as follows:

```
<xsl:with-param
   name="variable_name"
   select="expression"
>value</xsl:with-param>
```

name

This attribute identifies the parameter whose value will be replaced by the value that either the **select** attribute or the **value** attribute defines.

select

This attribute contains an expression that produces the variable value.

value

If you do not define the **select** attribute, the value attribute contains the variable value.

Example

This example defines a parameter and passes it to the site template.

```
<?xml version="1.0" encoding="UTF-8"?>
<xsl:stylesheet version="1.1"
xmlns:xsl="http://www.w3.org/1999/XSL/Transform">
   <xsl:attribute-set name="noborder">
     <xsl:attribute name="style">{text-decoration:none}
     </xsl:attribute>
     <xsl:attribute name="href"><xsl:value-of select=
     "address"/></xsl:attribute>
   </xsl:attribute-set>
   <xsl:template match="/">
     <xsl:element name="favorites">
        <xsl:for-each select="favorites/site">
          <xsl:call-template name="site">
<!-- passing a parameter to the site element template -->
             <xsl:with-param name="label">Site:
             </xsl:with-param>
          </xsl:call-template>
        </xsl:for-each>
     </xsl:element>
                                                  .../...
```

Managing and formatting data

```
.../...
   </xsl:template>
   <xsl:template match="site" name="site">
<!-- default value of the parameter -->
      <xsl:param name="label">Company: </xsl:param>
      <xsl:value-of select="$label"/>
      <xsl:element name="a" use-attribute-sets="noborder">
         <xsl:value-of select="text()"/>
      </xsl:element>
      <br/>
   </xsl:template>
</xsl:stylesheet>
```

This example defines the **label** parameter in the template that works with the **site** element. It initializes the value of this parameter with the word **Company:**.

The template that processes the document element includes an **<xsl:call-template>** element that calls the site template, passing the **label** parameter whose value has changed.

You can apply this XSL transformation to an XML document, such as the following:

```
<?xml version="1.0" encoding="ISO-8859-1" ?>
<?xml-stylesheet type="text/xsl" href="param.xsl"?>
<favorites>
   <site>ENI Publishing
      <address>http://www.eni-publishing.com</address>
   </site>
   <site>ENI Consulting
      <address>http://www.eni-consulting.com</address>
   </site>
</favorites>
```

Implementing XML

Here is the result in a browser:

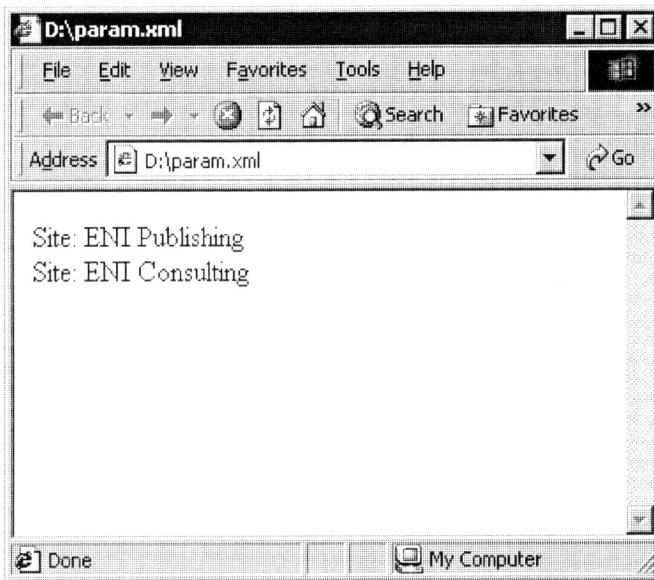

3. Summary example

This example combines many of the elements covered in this chapter.

This example produces a list of audio CDs. It comprises a DTD, an XML document, a CSS style sheet and an XSL style sheet.

DTD

```
<?xml version="1.0" encoding="UTF-8"?>
<!ELEMENT cd.list (page.title, cd+)>
<!ELEMENT cd (artist, title, spec)>
<!ELEMENT page.title (#PCDATA)>
<!ELEMENT artist (#PCDATA)>
<!ELEMENT title (#PCDATA)>
<!ATTLIST title
    original.title CDATA #IMPLIED
>
<!ELEMENT spec EMPTY>
<!ATTLIST spec
    type (Soundtrack | Live | Compilation | Studio) "Studio"
    nb_cd CDATA "1"
>
<!ENTITY KJ "Keith Jarrett">
```

The CD list comprises a page title and one or more CDs. Each CD comprises an artist, a title and a specification.

The artist and the title are defined as character strings. The title has an additional attribute that is used to define any original title. The specification comprises two attributes:

– album type: Soundtrack, Live, Compilation or Studio (default value),

– number of CDs in the album: this is **1**, by default.

XML document

```
<?xml version="1.0" encoding="ISO-8859-1" standalone="no"?>
<!DOCTYPE cd.list SYSTEM "cd_lists.dtd">
<?xml-stylesheet type="text/xsl" href="cd_lists.xsl"?>
<cd.list>
   <page.title>CD list</page.title>
                                                      .../...
```

```
.../...
   <cd>
      <artist>&KJ;</artist>
      <title>The Köln Concert</title>
      <spec type="Live"/>
   </cd>
   <cd>
      <artist>&KJ;</artist>
      <title>Dark Intervals</title>
      <spec/>
   </cd>
   <cd>
      <artist>Eric Clapton</artist>
      <title>Rush</title>
      <spec type="Soundtrack"/>
   </cd>
   <cd>
      <artist>U2</artist>
      <title>Rock's Hottest Ticket</title>
      <spec type="Live" nb_cd="2"/>
   </cd>
   <cd>
      <artist/>
      <title original.title="Phenomenon">Phenomena</title>
      <spec type="Soundtrack"/>
   </cd>
</cd.list>
```

CSS style sheet

```
BODY
{
    FONT-WEIGHT: normal;
    FONT-SIZE: 10pt;
    FONT-FAMILY: verdana
}
                                                        .../...
```

```
.../...
.pagetitle
{
    FONT-WEIGHT: bolder;
    FONT-SIZE: 13pt;
    COLOR: #000080
}
.artist
{
    FONT-WEIGHT: bolder;
    COLOR: #000080
}
.title
{
}
.originaltitle
{
    FONT-STYLE: italic
}
```

XSL style sheet

```
<?xml version="1.0" encoding="UTF-8"?>
<xsl:stylesheet version="1.0"
xmlns:xsl="http://www.w3.org/1999/XSL/Transform">
   <xsl:output indent="yes" encoding="ISO-8859-1"/>
   <xsl:key name="CDs-by-artist" match="cd" use="artist"/>
   <xsl:template match="/">
     <html>
       <head>
         <link rel="stylesheet" type="text/css"
         href="cd_lists.css"/>
         <title>CD list</title>
       </head>
       <body>
         <xsl:apply-templates select="cd.list"/>
                                              .../...
```

Implementing XML

```
.../...
        </body>
      </html>
  </xsl:template>
 ·<xsl:template match="cd.list">
      <div class="pagetitle">
      <xsl:value-of select="page.title"/>
  </div>
  <hr/>
  <br/>
  <xsl:for-each select="key('CDs-by-artist',
  /cd.list/cd/artist)">
      <xsl:sort order="ascending" select="artist"/>
      <xsl:sort order="ascending" select="title"/>
      <xsl:apply-templates/>
  </xsl:for-each>
</xsl:template>
<xsl:template match="page.title">
  <div class="pagetitle">
      <xsl:value-of select="."/>
  </div>
  <br/>
</xsl:template>
<xsl:template match="cd">
  <xsl:apply-templates/>
</xsl:template>
<xsl:template match="artist">
  <div class="artist">
      <xsl:if test="../spec[@type='Soundtrack']">Soundtrack
      <xsl:if test=".!=''">
        <br/>composed by: </xsl:if>
      </xsl:if>
      <xsl:if test=".!=''">
        <xsl:value-of select="."/>
      </xsl:if>
      <xsl:if test="../spec[@type='Live']"> in Concert
      </xsl:if>
                                                .../...
```

```
.../...
    </div>
    <xsl:choose>
        <xsl:when test=".='Keith Jarrett'">Jazz pianist
        </xsl:when>
        <xsl:otherwise/>
    </xsl:choose>
  </xsl:template>
  <xsl:template match="title">
    <div class="title">
        <xsl:value-of select="."/>
    </div>
   <xsl:if test="@original.title">
        <div class="originaltitle">
            <xsl:text>Original title: </xsl:text>
            <xsl:value-of select="@original.title"/>
        </div>
   </xsl:if>
   <xsl:value-of select="../spec/@nb_cd"/> CD
   <xsl:if test="../spec[@nb_cd>1]">s</xsl:if>
   <br/>
   <br/>
  </xsl:template>
</xsl:stylesheet>
```

This example uses XSLT version 1.0.

This style sheet contains three first-level element types: an element type to manage certain transformation characters (**<xsl:output>**), an element type to define a node set (**<xsl:key>**) and an element type to define a transformation template (**<xsl:key>**).

The **<xsl:output>** element indicates that the transformation tree uses the Western European character set (ISO-8859-1) and that the result of the transformation must be indented (at the time of writing, this element was unreliable in certain circumstances).

The **<xsl:key>** element associates the name **CDs-by-artist** with a CD set selected according to the artist.

This example defines four templates: to process the document element, the **cd.list** element, the **artist** element and the **title** element.

The template associated with the document element generates the HTML framework. This HTML framework contains a link to a CSS style sheet, to a title and to an **<xsl:apply-templates>**, which allows the rest of the document to be processed.

The template associated with the **cd.list** element starts by displaying the title of the page with which the **page.title** style is associated. Next, the template loops on the CD set that the **key()** function selects (this function uses the **<xsl:key>** element: this example selects all the CDs). This loop sorts the data that the remaining templates generate according to two conditions: the value of the **artist** element and the value of the **title** element.

The template that processes the **artist** element tests and displays a number of items. The first test examines the value of the current **cd** element. If the test result is "true", the CD is a soundtrack. In this case, if the artist is indicated, the template displays the text "composed by:" before the artist character string.

If it is present, the artist's name is always displayed, directly by the **artist** type class.

If the CD is **Live**, the phrase "in Concert" appears after the artist name.

The final action of this template indicates the instrument the artist plays.

The last template works with the **title** element. First it displays the title associated with the **title** type class. Next, this template tests and possibly displays the **original.title** attribute (which is associated with the **originaltitle** type class). Finally, the template displays the number of CDs followed by the word **CD**. If this number is greater than **1**, the letter **s** is suffixed to the word **CD**.

Here is the result in a browser:

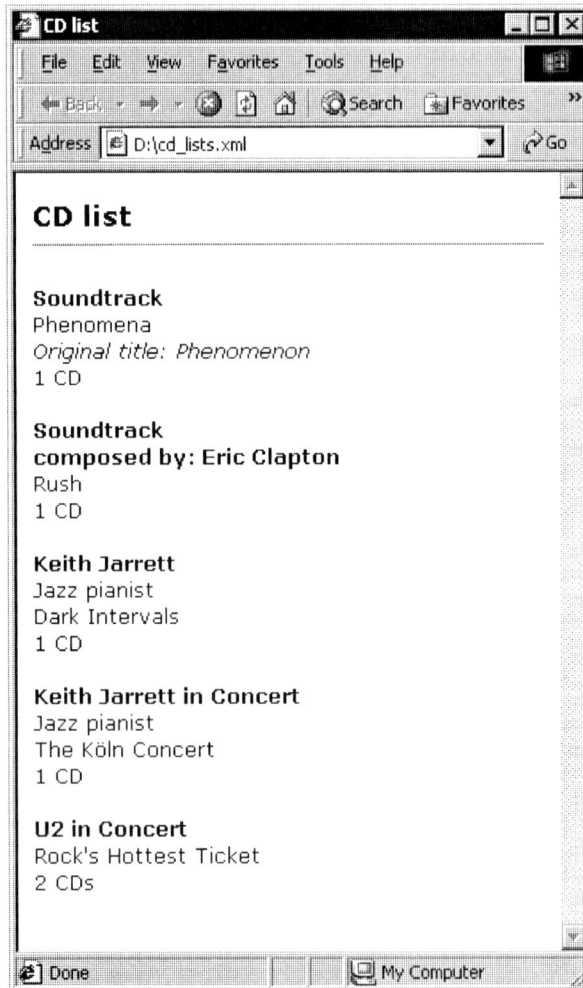

Chapter 5: XPath

Implementing XML

A. Introduction

As its name suggests, XPath provides an access path that allows you to navigate within XML documents.

To this end, XPath provides a number of features that allow you to process character strings, booleans and numbers.

The XPath specification is mainly associated with XSLT.

XPath models the XML document as a node tree. XPath defines different types of node: element nodes, attribute nodes or text nodes. To help you to use its features, XPath provides a mechanism to compute a character string value for each type of node.

XPath syntax is based on expressions. An XPath expression produces an object, of which there are four types:

– Boolean

– Number

– String

– Node-set

The evaluation of each expression depends on the current context.

One of the most important XPath expressions is the **location path**. The location path expression selects a set of nodes with respect to the context node.

B. Location paths

A location path can be relative or absolute. An absolute location path always begins with a slash (/), which signifies the root of the XML document. Otherwise, the starting node is the current context node.

Location path syntax can be abbreviated or unabbreviated. However, all the unabbreviated syntax elements do not have an abbreviated equivalent.

A location path has three parts:

- an axis, which defines the relationship between the context node and the nodes that the step selects,
- a node test, which specifies the node type and expanded name of the nodes that the step selects,
- zero or more predicates, which further refine the set of nodes that the step selects.

Location path syntax comprises the axis name, followed by a double-colon (::), followed by a node test, followed by zero or more expressions, each of which is contained between square brackets ([ ]).

Here is an example of a location path:

```
child::para[position()=1]
```

In this example, **child** is the name of the axis, **para** is the type of node the path selects and **[position()=1]** is a predicate.

You can analyze this syntax from left to right. In this example, the location step looks in the current node for the para node that is the first of its type.

1. Axes

XPath provides the following axes:

child

> contains the direct children of the context node.

descendant

> contains the descendants of the context node: a descendant can be a child or the child of a child and so forth.

parent

> contains the parent of the context node (if it has one).

ancestor

> contains the ancestors of the context node: an ancestor can be a parent or a parent's parent and so forth.
>
> The ancestor axis always contains the root node, unless the context node is the root node.

following-sibling

> contains all the context node's siblings that come after it: this axis is empty if the context node is an attribute or a namespace node.

preceding-sibling

> contains all the context node's siblings that come before it: this axis is empty if the context node is an attribute or a namespace node.

following

contains all nodes in the same document as the context node that come after it in the document order, excluding any descendants, attribute nodes and namespace nodes.

preceding

contains all nodes in the same document as the context node that come before it in the document order, excluding any descendants, attribute nodes and namespace nodes.

attribute

contains the attributes of the context node: this axis is empty when the context node is not an element.

namespace

contains the namespace nodes of the context node: this axis is empty when the context node is not an element.

self

contains only the context node.

descendant-or-self

contains the context node and its descendants.

ancestor-or-self

contains the context node and its ancestors: this axis always contains the root node.

2. Predicates

A predicate contains an expression. Each expression generates a boolean. For example:

para[3] is equivalent to **para[position()=3]**

Each of these expressions generates a boolean. The first expression does not carry out any tests: it simply selects the third element and is necessarily true. The second expression tests the position of the **para** element: it is **true** when this element is in the third position.

3. Unabbreviated syntax

child::para

  selects the **para** element that is a child of the context node.

child::*

  selects all the child elements of the context node.

child::text()

  selects all the **text** nodes of the context node.

child::node()

  selects all the child nodes of the context node, whatever their types.

attribute::name

  selects the **name** attribute of the context node.

attribute::*

selects all the attributes of the context node.

descendant::para

selects all the **para** descendants of the context node.

ancestor::div

selects all the **div** ancestors of the context node.

ancestor-or-self::div

selects all the **div** ancestors of the context node and the context node itself, if the context node is a **div** element.

descendant-or-self::para

selects all the **para** descendants of the context node and the context node itself, if the context node is a **para** element.

self::para

selects the context node itself, if it is a **para** element: otherwise, it selects nothing.

child::chapter/descendant::para

selects the **para** descendants of the **chapter** child of the context node.

child::*/child::para

selects the **para** grandchildren of the context node.

/

selects the document root (which is always the parent of the **document** element).

/descendant::para

selects all the descendant **para** elements in the same document as the context node.

/descendant::olist/child::item

selects all the **item** elements that have an **olist** parent and that are in the same document as the context node.

child::para[position()=1]

selects the first **para** child of the context node.

child::para[position()=last()]

selects the last **para** child of the context node.

child::para[position()=last()-1]

selects the next to last **para** child of the context node.

child::para[position()>1]

selects all the **para** children of the context node except for the first one.

following-sibling::chapter[position()=1]

selects the next **chapter** sibling of the context node.

preceding-sibling::chapter[position()=1]

selects the preceding **chapter** sibling of the context node.

/descendant::figure[position()=42]

selects the 42nd **figure** element of the document.

/child::doc/child::chapter[position()=5]/
child::section[position()=2]

selects the 2nd **section** of the 5th **chapter** element of the **doc** element in the document.

child::para[attribute::type="warning"]

selects all the **para** children of the context node that have a **type** attribute whose value is **warning**.

child::para[attribute::type='warning'][position()=5]

selects the 5th **para** child of the context node that has a **type** attribute whose value is **warning**.

child::para[position()=5][attribute::type="warning"]

selects the 5th **para** child of the context node, if this child has a **type** attribute value of warning.

child::chapter[child::title='Introduction']

selects the **chapter** child of the context node that has one or more **title** children that have a string value of **Introduction**.

child::chapter[child::title]

selects the **chapter** child of the context node that has one or more **title** children.

child::*[self::chapter and self::subtitle]

selects all the **chapter** and **subtitle** children of the context node.

child::*[self::chapter or self::subtitle]
[position()=last()]

> selects the last **chapter** or **subtitle** child of the context node.

4. Abbreviated syntax

para

> selects the **para** children elements of the context node.

*

> selects all the children of the context node.

text()

> selects all the **text** type children nodes of the context node.

name

> selects the **name** attribute of the context node.

@*

> selects all the attributes of the context node.

para[1]

> selects the first **para** child of the context node.

para[last()]

> selects the last **para** child of the context node.

*/para

selects all the **para** grandchildren of the context node.

/doc/chapter[5]/section[2]

selects the 2nd **section** of the 5th **chapter** of **doc**.

chapter//para

selects the **para** descendants of the **chapter** children of the context node.

//para

selects all the **para** descendants that the document root contains.

//olist/item

selects all the **item** elements that have an **olist** parent that is a descendant of the document root.

.

selects the context node.

.//para

selects the **para** descendants of the context node.

..

selects the parent of the context node.

../@lang

selects the **lang** attribute of the context node.

Implementing XML

para[@type="warning"]

selects all the **para** children of the context node that have a **type** attribute containing the value **warning**.

para[@type="warning"][5]

selects the 5th **Para** child of the context node that has a **type** attribute containing the value **warning**.

para[5][@type="warning"]

selects the 5th **para** child of the context node, provided that it has a **type** attribute with the value **warning**.

chapter[title="Introduction"]

selects the **chapter** children of the context node that have at least one **title** child containing the value **Introduction**.

chapter[title]

selects the **chapter** children of the context node that have at least one **title** child.

employee[@secretary and @assistant]

selects all the **employee** children of the context node that have both a **secretary** attribute and an **assistant** attribute.

C. Basic functions

XPath provides a large number of functions. These functions concern four object categories: node, string, boolean and number.

Each function can have zero or more arguments. A question mark (?) following an element indicates that the element is optional.

1. Processing nodes

```
number last()
```

This function returns a number equal to the index of the last node in the current context (context size).

```
number position()
```

This function returns a number equal to the context position of the node in the current context.

```
number count(node-set)
```

This function returns the number of nodes in the node-set passed in the argument.

```
node-set id (object)
```

This function selects the elements by their unique identifiers.

```
id("id1")
```

This function selects the element whose unique identifier is **id1**.

```
id("id1")/child::para[position()=5]
```

This function selects the 5th **para** child of the element whose unique identifier is **id1**.

```
string local-name (node-set?)
```

This function returns the local part of the expanded name of the node in the argument node-set that is the first node in the document order (the expanded name comprises a local part and a namespace URI). If the node-set passed in the argument is empty, or if the first node has no expanded name, this function returns an empty string.

If you omit the argument, it defaults to a node-set whose sole member is the context node.

```
string namespace-uri (node-set?)
```

This function returns the namespace URI of the expanded name of the node in the argument node-set that is the first node in the document order. If the node-set passed in the argument is empty, or if the first node has no expanded name or if the namespace URI is empty, this function returns an empty string. If you omit the argument, it defaults to a node-set whose sole member is the context node.

```
string name (node-set?)
```

This function returns a string value representing the expanded name of the node in the node-set passed as an argument that is the first node in the document order.

2. Processing strings

```
string string (object?)
```

This function converts its argument object into a string according to the following rules:

- A node-set converts to the string value of the first node in the document order. If the node-set is empty, this function returns an empty string.
- A number converts to a string as follows:

  Not a Number converts to the string **NaN**.

  Positive or negative zero converts to the string **0** (zero character).

  Positive infinity converts to the string **Infinity**.

  Negative infinity converts to the string **-Infinity**.

  An integer converts to a decimal form, as a number with no decimal point or leading zeros: a negative integer is preceded by a minus sign (-).

  If the number is not an integer, it converts to a number with a decimal point, with at least one digit before the decimal point and at least one digit after the decimal point: if the number is negative, it is preceded by a minus sign (-).

  The boolean **false** value converts to the string **false**. The boolean **true** value converts to the string **true**.

- Any object of a type other than the four basic types, converts to a string whose value depends on the type concerned.

If you omit the argument, it defaults to a node-set whose sole member is the context node.

⊙ The strings the **string** function produces are not intended for presentation to users. The **format-number** function and the (XSLT) **xsl:number** element provide this feature.

`string` **`concat`** `(string, string, string *)`

This function concatenates the argument strings.

`boolean` **`starts-with`** `(string, string)`

If the first argument string starts with the second argument string, this function returns the boolean value **true**. Otherwise it returns the boolean value **false**.

`boolean` **`contains`** `(string, string)`

If the first argument string contains the second argument string, this function returns the boolean value **true**. Otherwise it returns the boolean value **false**.

`string` **`substring-before`** `(string, string)`

This function returns the substring of the argument string that precedes the first occurrence of the second argument string in the first argument string. If the first argument string does not contain the second argument string, this function returns an empty string.

For example:
`substring-before("2001/04/01","/")`
will return 2001.

`string` **`substring-after`** `(string, string)`

This function returns the substring of the first argument string that comes after the first occurrence of the second argument string in the first argument string. If the first argument string does not contain the second argument string, this function returns an empty string.

For example:

```
substring-after("2001/04/01","/")
```

will return 04/01.

```
substring-after("2001/04/01","20")
```

will return 01/04/01.

`string` **substring** `(string, number, number?)`

This function returns the substring of the first argument string that starts at the position that the second argument specifies with the length that the third argument specifies.

For example:

```
substring("12345", 2, 3)
```

will return 234.

If you omit the third argument, this function returns the substring of the first argument string that starts at the position that the second argument specifies (and that ends at the end of the first argument string).

For example:

```
substring("12345",2)
```

will return 2345.

`number` **string-length** `(string?)`

This function returns the number of characters that the argument string contains.

If you omit the argument, it defaults to the string value of the context node.

`string` **normalize-space** `(string?)`

This function returns the argument string after normalizing its whitespace content.

If you omit the argument, it defaults to the string value of the context node.

```
string translate (string, string, string)
```

This function returns the first argument string after replacing any occurrences of the characters in the second argument string with the characters in the corresponding positions of the third argument string.

For example:
```
translate("test", "ts", "TS")
```
will return the string TeST.

If the third argument string is shorter than the second argument string, this function will remove the extra characters at the end of the second argument from the first argument string.

3. Processing booleans

```
boolean boolean (object)
```

This function converts its argument object into a boolean value according to the following rules:

- a number converts to **true**, unless it is negative, equal to zero or a NaN (Not a Number),
- a node-set converts to **true**, unless it is empty,
- a string converts to **true**, unless it has zero length.

```
boolean not (boolean)
```

This function inverses the boolean value of the argument: if the argument is **true**, it returns **false** and if the argument is **false**, it returns **true**.

```
boolean true ()
```

This function returns the boolean value **true**.

```
boolean false ()
```

This function returns the boolean value **false**.

```
boolean lang (string)
```

This function tests the **string** argument with respect to the **xml:lang** attribute of the context node. If the context node does not contain an attribute of this type, this function uses the context node's nearest ancestor that has an **xml:lang** attribute. This function returns true if the **xml:lang** attribute value is either the same as the argument language or is a sublanguage of the argument language. Otherwise, it returns **false**.

4. Processing numbers

```
number number (object?)
```

This function converts its argument object into a number according to the following rules:

- a boolean **true** converts to 1,
- a boolean **false** converts to 0,
- a string containing digits converts to the number that is nearest to the mathematical value that the string represents: it will take into account any leading sign and will ignore whitespace; on the other hand, if the string is not well formed (if it contains alphabetical characters, for example) this function will convert it into a **NaN**,
- a node-set argument is automatically converted to a string before it is passed to this function.

If you omit the argument, it defaults to the string value of the context node.

`number` **sum** `(node-set)`

> This function returns the sum of all the nodes in the argument node-set, after converting the string value of each of these nodes into a number.

`number` **floor** `(number)`

> This function returns the largest integer that is smaller than or equal to the argument number.

`number` **ceiling** `(number)`

> This function returns the smallest integer that is greater than or equal to the argument number.

`number` **round** `(number)`

> This function returns the nearest integer to the argument number:
>
> - if the argument is not a number, this function returns the string **NaN**,
> - if the argument is positive zero, this function returns positive zero,
> - if the argument is negative zero, this function returns negative zero.

Chapter 6: Developing

Implementing XML

As the preceding chapters indicate, XML is not yet fully adapted for client-side use with the Internet. As Internet Explorer 5 is the only browser currently able to make XSL/XSLT transformations to XML documents, it is not yet feasible to develop a client-side XML application for the Internet. On the other hand, working with an intranet is a different matter: when you can specify the browsers and the XML interpreter settings on your client machines, there is nothing to stop you from developing XML applications.

In any case, XML is not intended to work with a specific application. You cannot create a generic processing framework, as each XML document requires its own processing structure. However, what these different documents do have in common is the means of handling their processing structures: the **parser**.

The term parser comes from the field of development languages. The parser analyses the document structure and syntax. Moreover, it checks the correspondence between the entities in the XML document and any DTD associated with it.

When an XML application uses a parser it is connected to an API (Application Programming Interface) that contains the parser's properties, interfaces and constants.

There are two XML APIs, which differ in the way they approach the XML document.

The first API is called an event-driven API. It runs through the XML document from beginning to end and analyses each part of an element (opening tags, closing tags, attributes, contents, etc.). When it reaches a specific part of an element, it triggers an event associated with one of the application's functions. This API cannot navigate within the document. This "forward-only" technique allows the application to process large documents, as it reads them sequentially. This API is called **SAX** (**S**imple **A**PI for **X**ML).

The second API models the XML document as a node tree. The application can then process the different nodes using the functions that the API provides. This API is called **DOM** (**D**ocument **O**bject **M**odel).

A. Intranet and the Internet

In an intranet/Internet context, it is important to distinguish between two types of Web development: client-side development and server-side development.

Client-side applications always depend on the target browser. You can develop different types of client-side applications. One type of client-side application implements standard formatting, using CSS. Another type of client-side application is associated with extended formatting and provides access to the attributes and tests, using XSL. The following browsers support standard formatting: Internet Explorer 5, Netscape 6 and Opera 5. On the other hand, only Internet Explorer 5 supports XSL.

When you develop client-side applications, you do not need to concern your-self with the target browser. The Web server processes a server script as follows:

The client (a Web browser) connects to a Web server (via a telephone line or a company network, for example). Once it has connected, the client requests the Web site's page by default.

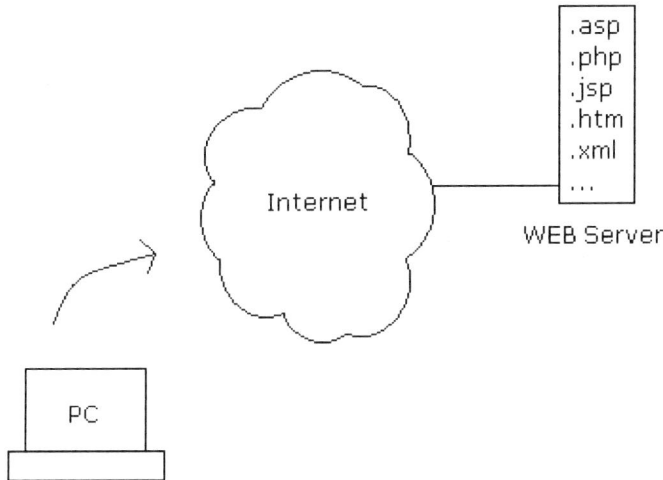

```
                                          .asp
                                          .php
                                          .jsp
                                          .htm
                   Internet               .xml
                                          ...
                                       WEB Server
        PC
```

If the Web server has a processing module for this page, it applies it. When an instruction generates HTML code, the server sends it to a virtual page (that corresponds only to the page the server is processing). When the server has finished processing the document, it sends this virtual HTML page to the browser on the client machine.

General principle

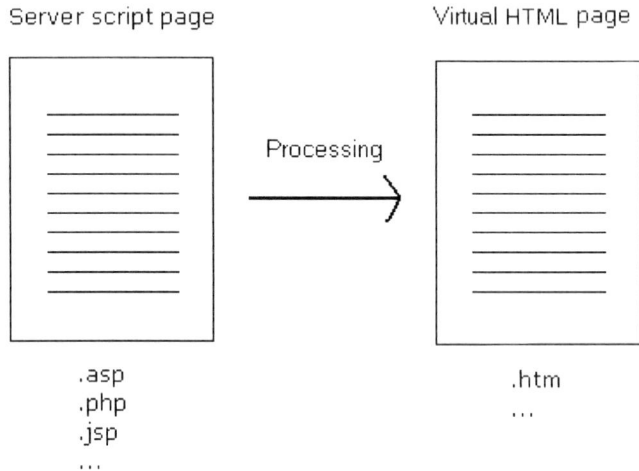

Server script page   Virtual HTML page

Processing

.asp   .htm
.php   ...
.jsp
...

If the Web server does not have a processing module for this type of page, it sends the page directly to the browser on the client machine. The result is similar to opening a (client or server) Web page in your browser from your hard disk (without using a Web server).

Only the name extension defines the type of the page you call.

1. Client-side XML

You can process a client-side XML document in several ways.

The preceding chapter describes the most important method: XSL (XSLT). In addition, you can use three other techniques: Data Source Object, Data Island and XSL with JavaScript.

a. Data Source Object

A Data Source Object, or DSO, makes the page on the client machine more dynamic, without the client needing to reload the page. This approach saves time and bandwidth (on the other hand, if the server were to run the same page, it would reload it). This process is called **data binding**.

DSO is based on the HTML tag **<xml>** (Internet Explorer).

You can use this element as follows:

```
<xml
   id="identifier"
   src="path_doc"
   async="boolean"
   validateonparse="boolean"
>
```

id

identifies the XML (or XSL) document for future use.

scr

if it is defined, this attribute indicates the access path and the name of the document that must be loaded.

async

indicates how the associated document must be loaded. If its value is **true** (its default value), the document must be loaded asynchronously; otherwise it must be loaded synchronously.

validateonparse

indicates whether or not the document must be validated when it is parsed: the default value is **true**.

The DSO technique divides up the document into records (like a database). The name of the database is that of the document element.

With the following XML document, the records correspond to the **cd** elements. Each record contains four fields: **artist**, **title**, **type** and **nbcd**.

```
<?xml version="1.0" encoding="ISO-8859-1" ?>
<cd.list>
  <cd>
     <artist>Keith Jarrett</artist>
     <title>The Köln Concert</title>
     <type>Live</type>
     <nbcd>1</nbcd>
  </cd>
  <cd>
     <artist>Keith Jarrett</artist>
     <title>Vienna Concert</title>
     <type>Live</type>
     <nbcd>1</nbcd>
  </cd>
  <cd>
     <artist>Keith Jarrett</artist>
     <title>Dark Intervals</title>
     <type>Studio</type>
     <nbcd>1</nbcd>
  </cd>
  <cd>
     <artist>Eric Clapton</artist>
     <title>Rush</title>
     <type>Soundtrack</type>
     <nbcd>1</nbcd>
  </cd>
                                          . . ./. . .
```

```
.../...
  <cd>
     <artist>U2</artist>
     <title>Rock's Hottest Ticket</title>
     <type>Live</type>
     <nbcd>2</nbcd>
  </cd>
  <cd>
     <artist/>
     <title>Phenomenon</title>
     <type>Soundtrack</type>
     <nbcd>1</nbcd>
  </cd>
</cd.list>
```

Example 1: simple display

This example reads the first **cd** element and displays it.

```
<html>
  <body>
     <H1>The first CD in the list</H1>
<!-- Loading the XML file and associating the ID xmldso -->
     <xml src="../cd_list.xml" id="xmldso" async="false"></xml>
     <br>Artist:
<!-- Reading the artist field in the first record -->
     <span datasrc="#xmldso" datafld="artist"></span>
     <br>Title:
     <span datasrc="#xmldso" datafld="title"></span>
  </body>
</html>
```

The **xml** tag loads the XML document and associates a unique identifier with it. The **span** tag allows you to select an XML document (**datasrc**) and the field you want to display (**datafld**).

Here is the result in a browser:

Example 2: navigating in a list

This example adds two buttons to the page. These buttons allow you to navigate in the CD list, displaying the CD's one by one. JavaScript functions manage these buttons.

```html
<html>
<head>
  <script language="JavaScript">
    function previous()
    {
<!-- Testing the position of the record pointer -->
      nav=xmldso.recordset
<!-- If the pointer is > 1, you can go backwards -->
      if (nav.absoluteposition > 1)
      {
        nav.moveprevious()
      }
    }

                                        .../...
```

Implementing XML

```
.../...
    function next()
    {
<!-- Testing the position of the record pointer -->
     nav=xmldso.recordset
<!-- If the pointer is < number of records, you can go
forwards -->
     if (nav.absoluteposition < nav.recordcount)
     {
         nav.movenext()
     }
    }
  </script>
</head>
<body>
  <H1>The CDs, one by one</H1>
  <xml src="../cd_list.xml" id="xmldso" async="false"></xml>
  <p>
    Title:
    <span datasrc="#xmldso" datafld="title"></span>
    <br>Artist:
    <span datasrc="#xmldso" datafld="artist"></span>
  </p><p>
<!-- Navigation buttons -->
    <input type="button" value="Previous CD"
    onclick="previous()">
    <input type="button" value="Next CD" onclick="next()">
  </p>
</body>
</html>
```

This example creates two functions to navigate in the CD list. These functions call DSO functions and properties. They start by selecting the recordset associated with the **xmldso** identifier. Next, they test the position of the current record to check if there is a previous record or a next record.

It would also have been possible to add a button to move directly to the first record (**movefirst()** function) or to move directly to the last record (**movelast()** function).

Here is the result in a browser:

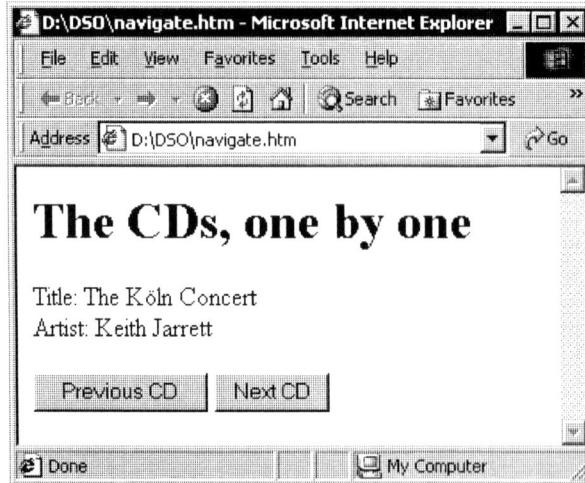

Example 3: creating a table whose data is stored in an XML document

This example uses the CD list to create a table.

```
<html>
  <body>
    <H1>The CDs listed in a table</H1>
    <xml src="../cd_list.xml" id="xmldso" async="false"></xml>
<!-- creating a table and associating it with a data source -->
    <table datasrc="#xmldso" width="100%" border="1">
      <thead>
        <th>Title</th>
        <th>Artist</th>
      </thead>
      <tr align="left">
        <td><span datafld="title"></span></td>
        <td><span datafld="artist"></span></td>
                                        .../...
```

Implementing XML

```
.../...
      </tr>
   </table>
  </body>
</html>
```

To create the table, this example declares the data source as an attribute of the **table** tag. It displays the data in the same way as the previous examples do: the **span** tag contains the **datafld** attribute, which contains the name of the field that must be displayed.

Here is the result in a browser:

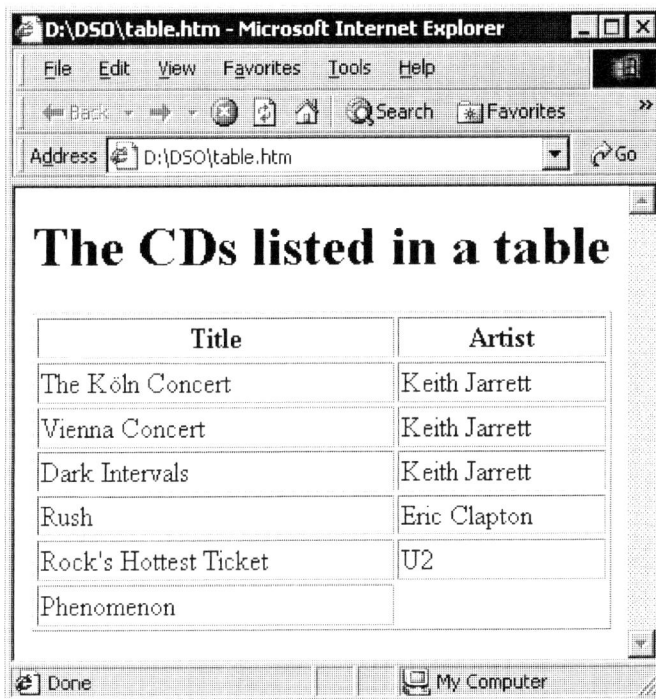

Example 4: dynamic features using JavaScript

The final DSO example illustrates the dynamic features you can add to a data source object using JavaScript.

```
<html>
<head>
  <script language="javascript">
    function showRecord(table)
    {
<!-- reading the ID of the row that was clicked -->
      var row=table.rowIndex
<!-- positioning the recordset on the ID read -->
      xmldso.recordset.absoluteposition =row
<!-- reading the data (title, artist, nbr CDs and type) -->
      TitleID.innerHTML =xmldso.recordset("title")
      ArtistID.innerHTML =xmldso.recordset("artist")
      idNbCD.innerHTML =xmldso.recordset("nbcd")
      TypeID.innerHTML =xmldso.recordset("type")
    }
  </script>
</head>
<body>
  <H1>CD table</H1>
  <xml id="xmldso" src="../cd_list.xml"></xml>
  <table datasrc="#xmldso" border="1">
    <thead>
      <tr align="left">
        <th>Title</th>
        <th>Artist</th>
      </tr>
    </thead>
    <tr align="left" onclick="showRecord(this)">
      <td><div datafld="title"></td>
      <td><div datafld="artist"></td>
                                    .../...
```

Implementing XML

```
.../...
      </tr>
   </table>
   <p><b>Click a CD to view its details</b>
   </p>
<!-- Creating a table to display the details -->
   <table border="1">
     <tr align="left"><th>Title:  </th>
     <td id="TitleID"></td></tr>
     <tr align="left"><th>Artist: </th>
     <td id="ArtistID"></td></tr>
     <tr align="left"><th>Type: </th>
     <td id="TypeID"></td></tr>
     <tr align="left"><th>Number of CDs: </th>
     <td id="idNbCD"></td></tr>
   </table>
</body>
</html>
```

This example displays the information in two parts: a general table showing the **Title** and **Artist** for all the CDs and a detail table showing this information for a specific CD plus the **Type** and the **Number of CDs**. When you click one of the table rows, you trigger the **showRecord()** function. This function assigns the values of the different fields to the detail table.

Here is the result in a browser:

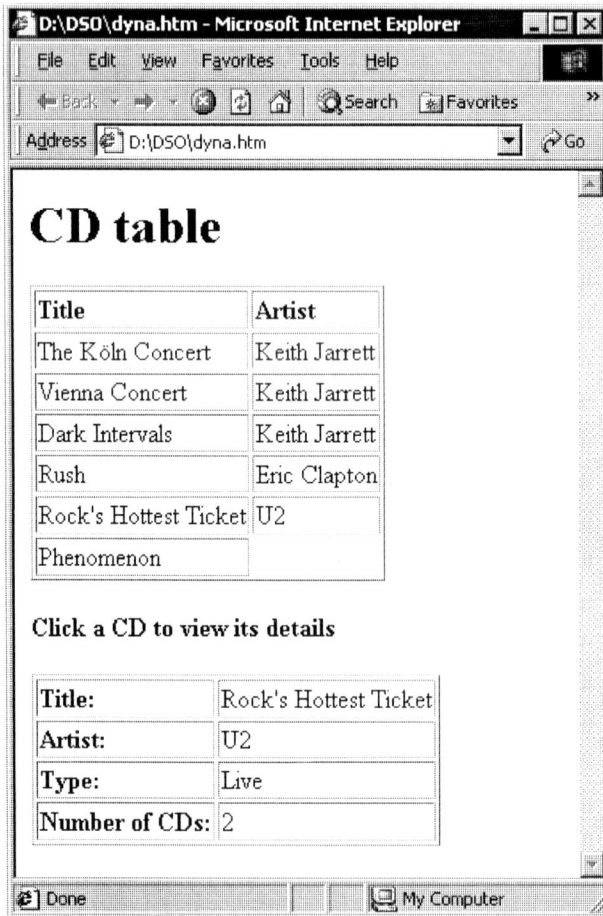

b. Data Island

A data island is an XML document inserted as a fragment of an HTML document. You can even associate an XSL document with a data island. Including XML data as a fragment of the HTML document can be convenient, as this means that you do not need a second file for the XML data. However, it also means that you cannot port your XML data outside the HTML document.

Implementing XML

Example of an XML document fragment

```
<html>
  <head>
    <title></title>
    <style type="text/css">
      BODY{FONT-FAMILY:verdana}
    </style>
    <xml id=docXML>
      <program_library>
        <program>
          <pname>Photoshop</pname>
          <editor>Adobe</editor>
        </program>
        <program>
          <pname>Illustrator</pname>
          <editor>Adobe</editor>
        </program>
        <program>
          <pname>Dreamweaver</pname>
          <editor>Macromedia</editor>
        </program>
      </program_library>
    </xml>
    <script language=javascript>
<!-- Creating the table dynamically -->
      txtPrograms = "<table><tr><th>Program</th>
      <th>Editor</th></tr>"
<!-- Reading the root of the XML document -->
      rootElem = docXML.documentElement
<!-- Reading the number of children (records) -->
      nbPrograms = rootElem.childNodes.length
<!-- Loop to create the table rows -->
      for (index=0; index<nbPrograms; index++){
        currentNode = rootElem.childNodes.item(index)
        pname = currentNode.selectSingleNode("pname")
        editor = currentNode.selectSingleNode("editor")
                                                    .../...
```

```
.../...
        txtPrograms += "<tr><td>"+pname.text+"</td>
        <td>"+editor.text+"</td></tr>"
    }
<!-- End of the table -->
    txtPrograms += "</table>"

    function display(){
<!-- Displaying the table -->
        listing.innerHTML = txtPrograms
    }
    </script>
  </head>
  <body  onload=display();>
    <H1>Program library</H1>
    <div id="listing"></div>
  </body>
</html>
```

This example uses the DOM functions and properties. The **xml** tag contains a fragment of XML document associated with an identifier. The JavaScript creates a temporary string. This string contains the table corresponding to the program library that the **xml** tag specifies.

A number of operations are necessary to build the table. This example assigns the root object of the XML fragment to the **rootElem** variable. Next, the number of programs is stored in the **nbPrograms** variable. The example then loops around all the programs, assigning a variable that points to the current node according to the index, via **childNodes.item(index)**. This technique allows each of the nodes to be read (using the **selectSingleNode()** function) along with the name of the program editor.

Here is the result in a browser:

Example of associating XML and XSL documents

HTML document:

```
<html>
  <head>
    <title></title>
    <style type="text/css">
      BODY{FONT-FAMILY:verdana}
      .preference{cursor:hand;font-weight:bold}
      .selection{cursor:hand}
    </style>
<!-- Loading an XML document -->
    <xml id=docXML src="data_is2.xml"></xml>
<!-- Loading an XSL document -->
    <xml id=docXSL src="data_is2.xsl"></xml>
    <script language=javascript>
                                                .../...
```

```
.../...
      function transform()
      {
        listing.innerHTML = docXML.transformNode
        (docXSL.XMLDocument);
      }
      function sort(condition)
      {
        sortField = docXSL.selectSingleNode
        ("//xsl:sort/@select");
        sortField.text = condition;
        transform();
      }
    </script>
  </head>
  <body onload=transform();>
    <H1>Program library</H1>
    <div id="listing"></div>
  </body>
</html>
```

This HTML document loads XML and XSL documents using **xml** tags. Next, it applies the XSL document to the XML document, via the **transformNode** function. A sort function is used. This function starts by locating the sort condition in the XSL document then it modifies this condition according to the parameter it receives as an argument.

Here is the XML document:

```
<?xml version="1.0"?>
<program_library>
  <program>
    <pname>Photoshop</pname>
    <editor>Adobe</editor>
    <pref>2</pref>
                                        .../...
```

```
.../...
    </program>
    <program>
      <pname>Illustrator</pname>
      <editor>Adobe</editor>
      <pref>5</pref>
    </program>
    <program>
      <pname>LiveMotion</pname>
      <editor>Adobe</editor>
      <pref>4</pref>
    </program>
    <program>
      <pname>Flash</pname>
      <editor>Macromedia</editor>
      <pref>3</pref>
    </program>
    <program>
      <pname>Dreamweaver</pname>
      <editor>Macromedia</editor>
      <pref>1</pref>
    </program>
</program_library>
```

Here is the associated XSL document:

```
<?xml version="1.0" encoding="UTF-8"?>
<xsl:stylesheet version="1.0"
xmlns:xsl="http://www.w3.org/1999/XSL/Transform">
    <xsl:template match="/">
      <span class="preference"
      onClick="sort('pref')" title="Sort
      according to the initial preference">Sort by
      preference</span>
      <br/>
      <br/>
      <table>
                                            .../...
```

```
.../...
        <tr>
<!-- Clicking one of the column headers sorts by the column -->
        <th class="selection"
        onClick="sort('pname')" title="Sort
        according to the program name">Program</th>
        <th class="selection"
        onClick="sort('editor')" title="Sort
        according to the editor">Editor</th>
        </tr>
<!-- Looping on each program and creating one row in the table
 per program -->
        <xsl:for-each select="/program_library/program">
          <xsl:sort select="pref" order="ascending"/>
          <tr>
            <xsl:apply-templates select="*"/>
          </tr>
        </xsl:for-each>
      </table>
    </xsl:template>
    <xsl:template match="*">
      <xsl:apply-templates select="*"/>
    </xsl:template>
    <xsl:template match="pname">
      <td>
        <xsl:value-of select="."/>
      </td>
    </xsl:template>
    <xsl:template match="editor">
      <td>
        <xsl:value-of select="."/>
      </td>
    </xsl:template>
 </xsl:stylesheet>
```

This XSL document creates a table containing the different values. It also defines the column headers as sensitive zones that allow you to sort the table when you click them.

Here is the result in a browser:

c. XSL and JavaScript

When you develop with JavaScript, you do not need an HTML document. All you need is an XML document, an XSL document and possibly a DTD and a CSS. The XML document contains only the data you want to process, while the XSL document contains the formatting instructions and the script that makes the contents dynamic.

Example of script associated with an XSL document

This example includes an XML document (CD list) and an XSL document. The XSL document allows you to carry out different sorts and make different selections (see the browser results at the end of the example). You can interact with the XML document as follows:

– when you click the name of an artist, the browser loads the document, selecting only this artist's CDs,

– you can use two choice lists: one of the lists allows you to select the CDs according to their type (Live, Soundtrack, Compilation or Studio); the other list allows you to sort the result according to different conditions (artist, title or type of CD),

– you can reset the selection (to show all the CDs sorted by artist) by clicking the text "All artists".

Here is the first block of script:

```
    <script for="window" event="onload">
      <xsl:comment>
        stylesheet = document.XSLDocument;
        source = document.XMLDocument;
<!-- Creating a pointer for the required information -->
        selectField = stylesheet.selectSingleNode
        ("//xsl:for-each/@select");
        sortField = stylesheet.selectSingleNode
        ("//xsl:sort/@select");
        selFieldLabel= stylesheet.selectSingleNode
        ("//div[@id='sel_label']");
        sortFieldLabel= stylesheet.selectSingleNode
        ("//span[@id='sort_label']");
      </xsl:comment>
    </script>
```

This first block of script identifies the XSL document fields, which you can easily modify. **selectField** and **sortField** allow you to change the sort order. **selectField** points to the **select** attribute of the XSL **for-each** instruction. In this example the **for-each** instruction allows you to define the node-set you want to select, via the **key** instruction. **sortField** points to the **select** attribute of the **sort** instruction, which sorts the selection results.

Here is the second block of script:

```
   <script language="javascript">
     <xsl:comment>
<!-- This function selects the CDs by artist -->
       function selectArtist(artist){
         selectField.value="key('CDs-by-artist', '"+artist+"')"
         updateSelInfo(artist+" CDs")
         update()
       }
<!-- This function selects the CDs by type and updates
the data -->
       function selectType(type){
         selectField.value="key('CDs-by-type', '"+type+"')"
         updateSelInfo(type+" CDs")
         update()
       }
<!-- Sort function -->
       function sort(type){
         sortField.value=type
         switch(type){
           case "artist": type="artist"
             break
           case "spec/@type": type="type"
             break
           default:
             break
         }
         updateSortInfo("sorted by "+type)
                                              .../...
```

```
.../...
        update()
      }
<!-- Initialization function -->
      function init(){
        selectField.value="key('CDs-by-artist',
        /List.CD/cd/artist)"
        updateSelInfo("All CDs")
        update()
      }
<!-- This function transforms the XML document with
the new parameters -->
      function update(){
        listing.innerHTML =
        source.documentElement.transformNode(stylesheet)
      }
      function updateSelInfo(selInfo){
        selFieldLabel.text = selInfo
      }
      function updateSortInfo(sortInfo){
        sortFieldLabel.text = sortInfo
      }
    </xsl:comment>
  </script>
```

This block of script includes all the selection and sort functions. The **select Artist** function selects the node-set corresponding to the artist name passed as an argument and updates the **selFieldLabel** pointer.

The **selectType** function selects the node-set corresponding to the type passed as an argument and also updates the **selFieldLabel** pointer.

The **sort** function sorts the selection according to the type passed as an argument and updates the **sortFieldLabel** pointer.

These three functions call the **update** function, which carries out a new transformation, taking these modifications into account.

The last two functions in this script block update the pointers to the selection and sort parameter fields.

The appendix of this book contains the complete XSL source document for this example.

You can associate an XML document with this example, such as the following:

```xml
<?xml version="1.0" encoding="ISO-8859-1" standalone="no"?>
<!DOCTYPE List.CD SYSTEM "cd_list.dtd">
<?xml-stylesheet type="text/xsl" href="cd_list.xsl"?>
<List.CD>
   <page.title>List of CDs</page.title>
   <cd>
     <artist>&KJ;</artist>
     <title>Vienna Concert</title>
     <spec type="Live"/>
   </cd>
   <cd>
     <artist>Eric Clapton</artist>
     <title>Rush</title>
     <spec type="SOUNDTRACK"/>
   </cd>
   <cd>
     <artist>U2</artist>
     <title>Rock's Hottest Ticket</title>
     <spec type="Live" nb_cd="2"/>
   </cd>
</List.CD>
```

Here is the result in a browser:

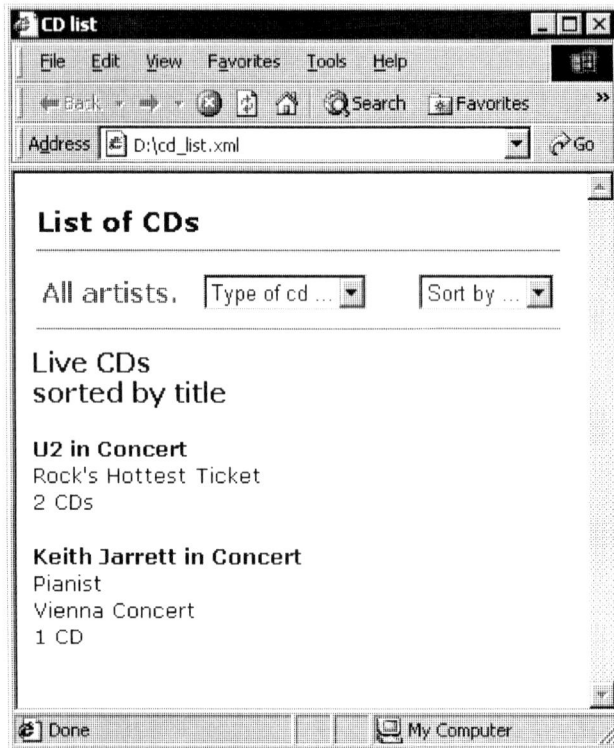

2. Server-side XML

This section describes two server-side XML methods: DOM and SAX. These methods use different languages: DOM uses ASP and SAX uses PHP. Each of the examples in this section uses a number of methods and functions that the corresponding API provides. The DOM and SAX sections of this chapter describe these APIs in greater detail.

a. ASP and DOM

DOM allows you to process XML documents in several ways. This section provides an XML-XSL transformation example and a list navigation example.

Both of these examples use the same XML document (in which the number of CDs can vary):

```
<?xml version="1.0" encoding="ISO-8859-1" standalone="no"?>
<!DOCTYPE cd.list SYSTEM "cd_lists.dtd">
<?xml-stylesheet type="text/xsl" href="cd_list.xsl"?>
<cd.list>
   <page.title>CD list</page.title>
   <cd>
     <artist>Keith Jarrett</artist>
     <title>Vienna Concert</title>
     <spec type="Live"/>
   </cd>
   <cd>
     <artist>Eric Clapton</artist>
     <title>Rush</title>
     <spec type="Soundtrack"/>
   </cd>
   <cd>
     <artist>U2</artist>
     <title>Rattle and Hum</title>
     <spec type="Compilation"/>
   </cd>
   <cd>
     <artist>U2</artist>
     <title>Rock's Hottest Ticket</title>
     <spec type="Live" nb_cd="2"/>
   </cd>
                                                           .../...
```

```
.../...
  <cd>
    <artist/>
    <title>Phenomenon</title>
    <spec type="Soundtrack"/>
  </cd>
</cd.list>
```

XML-XSL transformation example

```
<%
  set docXML = server.createobject("msxml2.DOMDocument.3.0")
  set docXSL = server.createobject("msxml2.DOMDocument.3.0")
  docXML.load (Server.MapPath("cd_list.xml"))
  docXSL.load (Server.MapPath("cd_list.xsl"))
%>
<html>
<head><title>XML and ASP</title></head>
<body>
<%
  Response.Write(docXML.transformNode (docXSL))
%>
</body>
</html>
```

This application is very useful for rapidly providing a simple XML and XSL document on the Internet.

First, this document sets the **docXML** and the **docXSL** objects as **msxml2.DOM-Document.3.0 server** objects.

Next, each of these objects loads a file (XML and XSL). **Server.MapPath** indicates that the file must be taken from the site hierarchy.

Finally, this document carries out the transformation and writes to the body of the HTML document.

Here is the associated XSL style sheet:

```
<?xml version="1.0" encoding="UTF-8"?>
<xsl:stylesheet version="1.0"
xmlns:xsl="http://www.w3.org/1999/XSL/Transform">
  <xsl:output indent="yes" encoding="UTF-16"/>
<!-- Creating selection keys -->
  <xsl:key name="CDs-by-artist" match="cd" use="artist"/>
  <xsl:key name="CDs-by-type" match="cd" use="spec/@type"/>
  <xsl:template match="/">
    <html>
      <head>
<!-- Adding a CSS -->
        <link rel="stylesheet" type="text/css"
        href="cd_lists.css"/>
        <title>CD list</title>
      </head>
      <body>
        <xsl:apply-templates select="list.cd"/>
      </body>
    </html>
  </xsl:template>
  <xsl:template match="*">
    <xsl:apply-templates/>
  </xsl:template>
  <xsl:template match="list.cd">
    <div class="pagetitle">
      <xsl:value-of select="page.title"/>
    </div>
    <br/>
<!-- Looping on each artist + sort -->
    <xsl:for-each select="key('CDs-by-artist',
    /list.cd/cd/artist)">
        <xsl:sort order="ascending" select="artist"/>
        <xsl:apply-templates/>
    </xsl:for-each>
  </xsl:template>
                                                      .../...
```

```
.../...
  <xsl:template match="page.title">
    <div class="pagetitle">
      <xsl:value-of select="."/>
    </div>
    <br/>
  </xsl:template>
  <xsl:template match="cd">
    <xsl:apply-templates/>
  </xsl:template>
  <xsl:template match="artist">
    <div class="artist">
<!-- If the type of the CD is Soundtrack, display the text
Original soundtrack -->
<!-- If the artist is not empty, display the text composer:
followed by the name of the artist -->
        <xsl:if test="../spec[@type='SOUNDTRACK']">
        Original soundtrack
          <xsl:if test=".!=''">
            <br/>Composer: </xsl:if>
        </xsl:if>
<!-- If the type of the CD is not Soundtrack, display
the artist -->
        <xsl:if test=".!=''">
          <span class="sel_artist"
          onclick="selectartist('{.}')">
            <xsl:value-of select="."/>
          </span>
        </xsl:if>
<!-- If the type of the CD is Live, display the text
in Concert -->
        <xsl:if test="../spec[@type='Live']"> in Concert
        </xsl:if>
      </div>
      <xsl:choose>
                                              .../...
```

Implementing XML

```
.../...
<!-- When the artist is Keith Jarrett, indicate that
he is a pianist -->
        <xsl:when test=".='Keith Jarret'">Pianist</xsl:when>
        <xsl:otherwise/>
      </xsl:choose>
  </xsl:template>
  <xsl:template match="titre">
      <div class="titre">
        <xsl:value-of select="."/>
      </div>
      <xsl:value-of select="../spec/@nb_cd"/> CD
<!-- Test the number of CDs, add an s to CD if this number is
greater than 1 -->
      <xsl:if test="../spec[@nb_cd>1]">s</xsl:if>
      <br/>
      <br/>
  </xsl:template>
</xsl:stylesheet>
```

Here is the result in a browser:

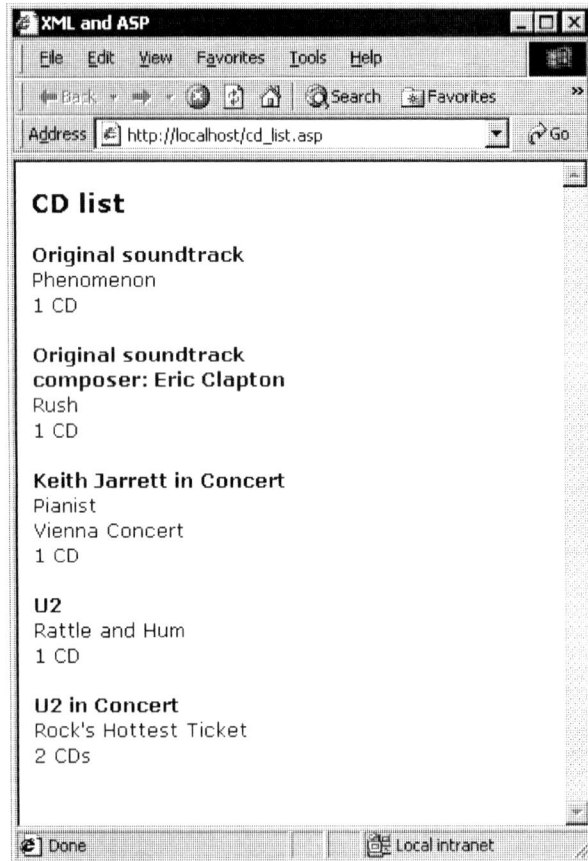

Navigation example

The following example allows you to navigate in a list of audio CDs. This example does not use any XSL style sheet. All you need in this case is the XML document and the ASP page. The DTD and the CSS style sheet are optional. The DTD allows you to manage default attribute values and the CSS style sheet enhances the display.

```
<%
  set docXML = server.createobject("msxml2.DOMDocument.3.0")
  docXML.load (Server.MapPath("cd_list.xml"))
%>
<html>
  <head>
    <title>XML and ASP</title>
    <link rel="stylesheet" href="cd_list.css" type="text/css">
  </head>
  <body>
    <table>
<%
<!-- Get the parameters received by the asp page -->
id = Request.QueryString("id")
dirn = Request.QueryString("dirn")
nbElts = docXML.documentElement.childNodes.length
<!-- Test the navigation possibilities -->
if (dirn="1")then
  id = id-1
  if id<1 then
    id = nbElts-1
  end if
elseif (dirn="2")then
  id = id+1
  if id>nbElts-1 then
    id = 1
                                                    .../...
```

```
.../...
   end if
else
   id = 1
end if
<!-- Select and copy the record fields corresponding
to the ID -->
artist = docXML.documentElement.childNodes.item(id)
.childNodes.item(0).text
title = docXML.documentElement.childNodes.item(id)
.childNodes.item(1).text
cdtype = docXML.documentElement.childNodes.item(id).
childNodes.item(2).attributes.item(0).text
nbcd = docXML.documentElement.childNodes.item(id)
.childNodes.item(2).attributes.item(1).text
<!-- Display this info and the navigation buttons -->
Response.Write "<tr><td colspan=2><span class=artist>"
& artist & "</span></td></tr>"
Response.Write "<tr><td colspan=2>" & title & "</td></tr>"
Response.Write "<tr><td>" & cdtype & "</td><td>" & nbcd
if nbcd < 2 then
   Response.Write " CD"
else
   Response.Write " CDs"
end if
   Response.Write "</td></tr>"
%>
    </table>
    <input type=button value="Previous" onclick
    ="window.location='cd_list2.asp?dirn=1&id=<%=id%>'">
    <input type=button value="Next" onclick
    ="window.location='cd_list2.asp?dirn=2&id=<%=id%>'"
    id=button1 name=button1>
  </body>
</html>
```

This example navigates by reloading the page.

It loads the XML document, associates it with docXML and tests the navigation direction. If the **dirn** variable is not assigned, the program concludes that this is the first visit to the ASP page and that the index of the CD to be displayed is **1** (**0** corresponds to the title element).

Next, the example displays the elements of the selected CD.

The example creates two navigation buttons: these buttons reload the page, passing the **id** and **dirn** arguments.

Here is the result in a navigator:

b. PHP and SAX

PHP provides two methods of processing an XML document. The first method generates an associated table that contains the complete XML document. PHP uses the **xml_parse_into_struct()** function for this purpose. PHP manages this table in a similar way to that in which DOM manages its hierarchy. The second method is the SAX event-driven method. The following example illustrates this second method.

Example:

```
<html>
  <head>
    <link rel="stylesheet" type="text/css"
    href="testxml.css"/>
    <title>Test XML and PHP</title>
  </head>
  <body>
    <span class=pagetitle>CD list in PHP</span>
    <br><br>
    <table>
<?
/* This function manages the contents of an element */
function cdataHandler($parser, $data){
  print($data);
}
/* This function runs when the parser starts an element */
function startElt($parser, $name, $attr){
  switch($name){
    default:
      print("<td>");
      break;
    case "CD":
      print("<tr>");
      break;
    case "ARTIST":
      print("<td><span class='sel_artist'>");
      break;
  }
}
/* This function runs when the parser gets to the end of
an element */
function endElt($parser, $name){
  switch($name){
    default:
      print("</td>");
                                            .../...
```

```
.../...
      break;
    case "CD":
      print("</tr>");
      break;
    case "NBCD":
      print(" CD</td>");
      break;
    case "ARTIST":
      print("</span></td>");
      break;
  }
}

/* Implementing the parser */
if (!($parser=xml_parser_create())){
  print("Error creating the parser.");
  exit();
}

/* Associating functions with events */
xml_set_character_data_handler($parser, "cdataHandler");
xml_set_element_handler($parser, "startElt", "endElt");

/* Opening an XML document */
if (!($fp=fopen("m:\cd_list.xml", "r")))
{
  print("Cannot open a file.");
  xml_parser_free($parser);
  exit();
}
/* While data is found in the XML document, it is sent in 1024
byte packets to the parser */
while($line=fread($fp, 1024))
{
  if(!xml_parse($parser, $line, feof($fp)))
  {
                                                        .../...
```

```
.../...
    print("Parser error.");
  }
}
xml_parser_free($parser);
?>
    </table>
  </body>
</html>
```

This example generates a table containing all the CDs in the XML document.

The example is composed of three parts:
– defining functions to manage the events,
– calling functions that associate events with functions,
– parsing the XML document.

In this second part, the first function called manages the text content of an element. The text to be processed is passed as an argument together with a reference to the management function concerned. The second function processes the start and end of element events. Its parameters are the name of the element, the name of the function the parser must run when it sees the beginning of the element and the function the parser must run when it sees the end of the element.

The first part defines the functions that this second part calls. The first of these functions, which manages the text content, just displays this content. The two other functions carry out the appropriate processing, according to the name of the element.

The third part manages the file, to parse the document by blocks of 1 KB (in this case).

Here is the result in a browser:

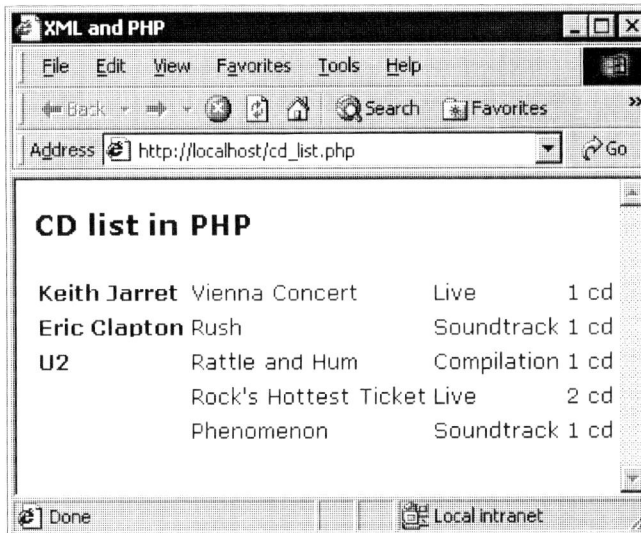

B. Visual Basic

To develop non-Internet applications, you can choose from a vast range of languages, such as assembly language, C, Java, Pascal, Basic and Cobol, for example.

Practically all applications have some external communication. This may concern exporting or importing a file or using a communications channel with another application. In almost all cases, such external links involve data exchange.

For this reason, most software editors are gradually integrating XML into their applications.

Managing and formatting data

As a semi-structured metalanguage, XML is very suitable for these data exchanges.

The following example manages an XML document in Visual Basic.

Application example

This application loads an XML document and displays its contents as a tree in a Treeview Control.

```
Option Explicit
Private oDoc As MSXML.DOMDocument
Private bLoaded As Boolean
Private bValidate As Boolean

Private Sub DisplayXMLTree()
  If bLoaded Then
    'Reset the Treeview
    tvwNodeTree.Nodes.Clear
    'Calling AddNode with the XML doc root as an argument
    AddNode oDoc.documentElement
  End If
End Sub

Private Function AddNode(ByRef oElem As MSXML.IXMLDOMNode,
Optional ByRef oTreeNode As Node)
  Dim oNewNode As Node
  Dim oNodeList As MSXML.IXMLDOMNodeList
  Dim i As Long

  If oTreeNode Is Nothing Then
    'Adding a node to the root of the Treeview
    Set oNewNode = tvwNodeTree.Nodes.Add
    oNewNode.Expanded = True
                                              .../...
```

Implementing XML

```
.../...
  Else
    'Adding a node under tvwChild in the Treeview
    Set oNewNode = tvwNodeTree.Nodes.Add(oTreeNode, tvwChild)
    oNewNode.Expanded = True
  End If

  Select Case oElem.nodeType
    Case MSXML.NODE_ELEMENT
      'If the node is a Node Element type,
      'get the attributes and display them
      If GetAttributes(oElem) <> "" Then
        oNewNode.Text = "<" & oElem.nodeName & " " &
        GetAttributes(oElem) & ">"
      Else
        oNewNode.Text = "<" & oElem.nodeName & ">"
      End If
      Set oNewNode.Tag = oElem
    'If the node is a Node Text type, display
    Case MSXML.NODE_TEXT
        oNewNode.Text = "Text: " & oElem.nodeValue
        Set oNewNode.Tag = oElem
    'If the node is a Node CData Section type, display
    Case MSXML.NODE_CDATA_SECTION
        oNewNode.Text = "CDATA: " & oElem.nodeValue
        Set oNewNode.Tag = oElem
    'If the node is another type, display type + value
    Case Else
        oNewNode.Text = oElem.nodeTypeString & ": " &
        oElem.nodeName
        Set oNewNode.Tag = oElem
  End Select

  'Select all the children of the current node and
  'add to the TreeView
  Set oNodeList = oElem.childNodes
                                          .../...
```

Managing and formatting data

```
.../...
  For i = 0 To oNodeList.length - 1
    AddNode oNodeList.Item(i), oNewNode
  Next i
End Function

Private Function GetAttributes(ByRef oElm
As MSXML.IXMLDOMNode) As String
  Dim sAttr As String
  Dim i As Long
  sAttr = ""

  For i = 0 To oElm.Attributes.length - 1
    sAttr = sAttr & oElm.Attributes.Item(i).nodeName & "='" &
    oElm.Attributes.Item(i).nodeValue & "' "
  Next i
  GetAttributes = sAttr
End Function

'Open an XML file
Private Sub cmdFileChoose_Click()
  dlgFileChoose.FileName = txtFile.Text
  dlgFileChoose.ShowOpen
  If Not dlgFileChoose.FileName = "" Then
    txtFile.Text = dlgFileChoose.FileName
    LoadXML
    DisplayXMLTree
  End If
End Sub

'Load the file and validate, if necessary
Private Sub LoadXML()
  Set oDoc = New DOMDocument
  oDoc.async = False

  If bValidate Then
    oDoc.validateOnParse = True
                                    .../...
```

```
.../...
  Else
    oDoc.validateOnParse = False
  End If
  oDoc.Load "file:///" & txtFile.Text
  If oDoc.parseError.errorCode = 0 Then
    bLoaded = True
  Else
    MsgBox oDoc.parseError.reason & vbCrLf &
    oDoc.parseError.Line & vbCrLf &
    oDoc.parseError.srcText
    bLoaded = False
  End If
End Sub

Private Sub optValidOff_Click()
  bValidate = False
End Sub

Private Sub optValidOn_Click()
  bValidate = True
End Sub
```

Here is what this application does, in chronological order:

First, it loads the XML document and validates it if the **On** option is selected in the **Validation** frame. Next, the **DisplayXMLTree** function starts building the tree. It adds each node using the **AddNode** function. If the node is an element type node, it calls the **GetAttributes** function and returns a string containing the attributes and their values. It tests three more types: text nodes, CDATA nodes and comments nodes. For other types, it carries out a default routine, which indicates the type of the node and any value it may have.

Here is the result of the application:

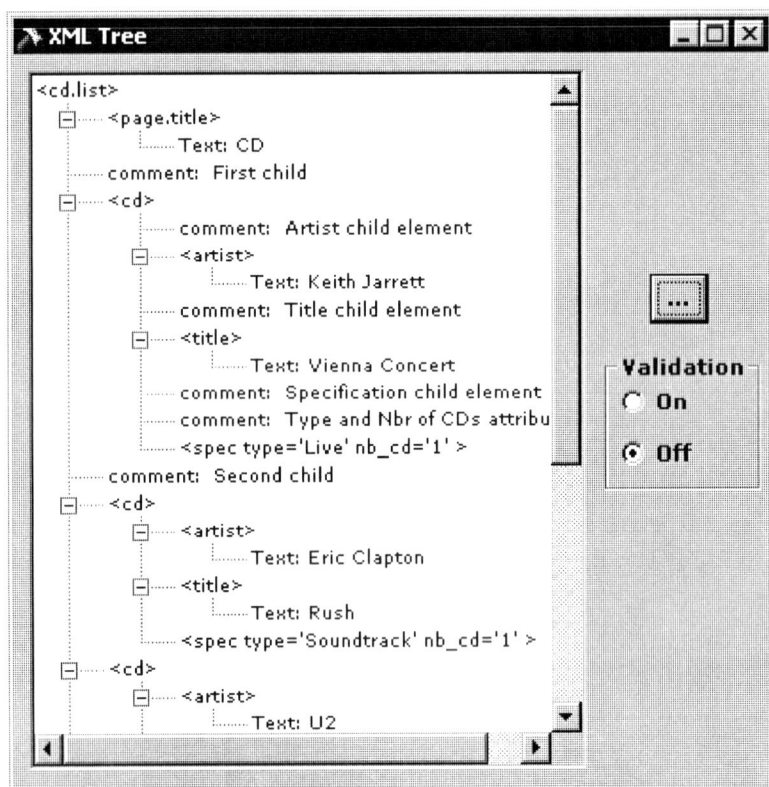

```
XML Tree                                    _ □ ✕

<cd.list>
  ⊟──── <page.title>
          └──── Text: CD
  ──── comment:  First child
  ⊟──── <cd>
          ──── comment:  Artist child element
          ⊟──── <artist>
                  └──── Text: Keith Jarrett
          ──── comment:  Title child element
          ⊟──── <title>
                  └──── Text: Vienna Concert
          ──── comment:  Specification child element
          ──── comment:  Type and Nbr of CDs attribu
          └──── <spec type='Live' nb_cd='1' >
  ──── comment:  Second child
  ⊟──── <cd>
          ⊟──── <artist>
                  └──── Text: Eric Clapton
          ⊟──── <title>
                  └──── Text: Rush
          └──── <spec type='Soundtrack' nb_cd='1' >
  ⊟──── <cd>
          ⊟──── <artist>
                  └──── Text: U2
```

Validation
  ○ On
  ⦿ Off

Implementing XML

C. DOM

DOM (Document Object Model) is an XML programming interface. It specifies how the XML document must be processed. XML DOM was designed for use with any programming language and on any operating system.

DOM allows you to create an XML document, to navigate within the document structure and to add, modify and delete elements.

DOM is based on the Node interface.

The XML parser loads an XML document into memory and you can then use DOM to handle its contents.

The highest level (root element) of the tree that represents the XML document is the **documentElement**. This element contains one or more **childNodes** that represent the branches of the tree.

The nodes are divided up into different types. DOM associates a **nodeName** and a **nodeValue** with each type. Internet Explorer 5 uses the **nodeTypeString** property to return the node type in the form of a string.

1. The different types of node

Type 1

Constant:	ELEMENT_NODE
nodeTypeString:	Element
nodeName:	tagName
nodeValue:	null

Type 2

Constant: ATTRIBUTE_NODE

nodeTypeString: Attribute

nodeName: name

nodeValue: value

Type 3

Constant: TEXT_NODE

nodeTypeString: Text

nodeName: #text

nodeValue: content of node

Type 4

Constant: CDATA_SECTION_NODE

nodeTypeString: cdatasection

nodeName: #cdatasection

nodeValue: content of node

Type 5

Constant: ENTITY_REFERENCE_NODE

nodeTypeString: entityreference

nodeName: entity reference name

nodeValue: null

Type 6

Constant:	ENTITY_NODE
nodeTypeString:	entity
nodeName:	entity name
nodeValue:	null

Type 7

Constant:	PROCESSING_INSTRUCTION_NODE
nodeTypeString:	processinginstruction
nodeName:	target
nodeValue:	content of node

Type 8

Constant:	COMMENT_NODE
nodeTypeString:	comment
nodeName:	#comment
nodeValue:	comment text

Type 9

Constant:	DOCUMENT_NODE
nodeTypeString:	document
nodeName:	#document
nodeValue:	null

Type 10

Constant:	DOCUMENT_TYPE_NODE
nodeTypeString:	documenttype
nodeName:	doctype name
nodeValue:	null

Type 11

Constant:	DOCUMENT_FRAGMENT_NODE
nodeTypeString:	documentfragment
nodeName:	#document fragment
nodeValue:	null

Type 12

Constant:	NOTATION_NODE
nodeTypeString:	notation
nodeName:	notation name
nodeValue:	null

2. Node object

This object represents any node in the node tree. A node can be any of the types defined above. All these node types have properties and methods. A selection of these properties and methods are described below:

Properties and methods marked with an asterisk (*) are specific to Internet Explorer.

Properties

attributes

returns an object containing all the attributes of the node.

basename *

returns the name of the node without the namespaces.

childNodes

returns a node list containing all the children of the current node.

dataType *

returns the type of data for this node.

firstChild

returns the first child of the node.

lastChild

returns the last child of the node.

nextSibling

returns the next sibling.

nodeName

returns the node name depending on the type.

nodeType

returns the number corresponding to the type.

nodeTypeString *

returns the type in the form of a string.

nodeValue

returns or assigns the value of the node, depending on the type.

ownerDocument

returns the root node of the document (document object).

parentNode

returns the parent of the node.

previousSibling

returns the previous sibling.

text *

returns the text for the current node and its children.

xml *

returns the xml (text and tags) for the current node and its children.

Methods

appendChild(newChild)

adds the **newchild** node, as the last child of the current node.

cloneNode(booleen)

returns a clone of the current node: if **boolean** is true, the clone contains all the children.

asChildNodes()

returns true if the node has at least one child.

insertBefore(newNode, refNode)

inserts a new child node before the **refNode**.

removeChild(childName)

removes the **childName** node.

replaceChild(newNode, oldNode)

replaces the **oldNode** with the **newNode**.

selectNodes(xpath) *

returns a **NodeList** corresponding to the specified **xpath**.

selectSingleNode(xpath) *

returns a node corresponding to the specified **xpath**.

transformNode(stylesheet) *

transforms the current node and its children using the specified style sheet.

transformNodeToObject(stylesheet, result) *

transforms the current node and its children using the specified style sheet. The **result** object stores the result of this operation.

3. NodeList object

This object represents a collection of nodes.

Properties

length

returns the number of nodes in the collection.

Methods

nextNode() *

returns the next node in the collection.

item()

returns a specific node in the collection.

reset() *

resets the pointer to the first node in the collection.

4. Document object

The **Document** object is the root of the tree. All the other nodes in the tree are children of this root node (**documentElement**).

Properties

documentElement

returns the root element of the document.

doctype

returns the name of the DTD.

Methods

createAttribute(attributeName)

creates an attribute with the name: **attributeName**.

createCDATASection(text)

creates a **CDATASection** object containing the specified **text**.

createComment(text)

creates a comment node containing the specified **text**.

createDocumentFragment()

creates an empty **documentFragment** object.

createElement(tagName)

creates an element with the name: **tagName**.

createEntityReference(refName)

creates an **EntityReference** object with the name: **refName**.

createProcessingInstruction(target, text)

creates a **ProcessingInstruction** object containing the specified **text** for the specified **target** application.

createTextNode(text)

creates a **TextNode** objet with the specified **text**.

getElementsByTagName(nodeName)

returns the specified node together with its children.

5. Element object

This object represents the element nodes of the document. If an element node contains text, this text is represented in a **TextNode** object.

Properties

TextNode

returns or assigns the name of a node.

Methods

getAttribute(attributeName)

returns the value of the specified attribute.

getAttributeNode(attributeName)

returns the **Attr** object of the specified **attributeName**.

getElementsByTagName(nodeName)

returns the specified node together with its children.

removeAttribute(attributeName)

removes the specified attribute: if the attribute has a default value, it is replaced by this value.

removeAttributeNode(attributeNode)

removes the specified **attributeNode**: if the **attributeNode** has a default value, it is replaced by this value.

setAttribute(attributeName, attributeValue)

inserts a new attribute with the specified name and value.

setAttributeNode(attributeNode)

inserts an attribute node with the name: **attributeNode**.

6. Attr object

This object represents an attribute of an object element. The **attr** object has the same properties and methods as a general node.

Properties

name

returns or assigns the name of an attribute.

specified

returns a boolean indicating whether or not the document defines the value of the attribute.

value

returns or assigns the value of an attribute.

7. Text object

This object represents the text an element contains, in the form of a node.

Methods

splitText(offset)

splits a **Text** node at the specified **Offset**.

8. CDATASection object

This object represents a **DATASection** mode in the document. In this node, you can store characters that would otherwise be considered as markup code (such as < and >).

9. Comment object

This object represents the contents of a comment in the document.

D.SAX

SAX (Simple API for Xml) is an event-driven data management method. SAX registers with the parser, event management functions for each object in an XML document (an event is the opening or closing of a tag, for example). These functions specify the number of arguments their templates require. They are called **callback** functions.

The names of the methods that assign functions to events can vary according to the parser used.

Here is a selection of these methods, which, as a general rule, always have the same objectives.

Methods

new()

creates a new SAX parser object.

start_document()

is called at the beginning of the document.

start_element()

is called at the beginning of an element: it receives several arguments including the name of the element.

characters()

is called for all the text content of an element.

end_element()

> is called at the end of an element: it receives several arguments including the name of the element.

end_document()

> is called at the end of the document.

processing_instruction()

> is called when a processing instruction is encountered: it receives several arguments including the name of the target application and any processing instruction data.

entity_reference()

> is called when an entity is encountered.

notation()

> is called when a notation is encountered.

parse()

> instructs the application to start parsing the document.

Chapter 7: New standards

This chapter describes the different applications that have appeared as a result of XML.

You can apply XML to a large number of fields. The behavior of an XML application depends mainly on the document definition (DTD (Document Type Definition) or XSD (eXtensible Shema Definition)) and on the field of application (multimedia, engineering, etc.).

This chapter does not aim to present all the existing applications: these are very numerous and some of them are still being developed.

This chapter describes applications in a wide range of fields, such as multimedia, security, data queries, content description, science and engineering and data sharing.

A. Multimedia

1. SVG

To transmit images on the Web, graphic bitmap formats are commonly used, such as GOF, JPEG (JPG) and PNG. Before SVG (Scalable Vector Graphics) appeared, only proprietary vector graphics formats were available. Flash (Macromedia) and QuickTime (Apple) are examples of such formats. The Adobe Company developed the SVG standard, which is currently undergoing the W3C ratification process.

SVG is based on XML and uses the same structure. An SVG document contains structured text that describes the image along with actions you associate with the image. This approach means that SVG documents use less disk space than corresponding JPG or GIF documents. The SVG format uses W3C standards, such as CSS and DOM.

As an SVG document uses vectors, it allows you to enlarge a zone without losing quality. It also allows you to port your images to other devices, such as personal organizers (with smaller screens) or printers (with paper formats), again without loss of quality.

Moreover, you can add scripts within your SVG document. As with HTML documents, you can manage events such as **onmouseover** and **onclick**, for example.

The programmable approach to displaying and printing in this format has aroused the interest of a considerable number of program editors. CSIRO (Commonwealth Scientific and Industrial Research Organisation) and IBM have developed an SVG viewer in Java. Adobe provides a plug-in that allows users of Netscape and Internet Explorer to view this format. Jasc Software offers the WebDraw application that allows you to view and edit SVG files. Adobe Illustrator (version 9.0) allows you to export files in SVG format and Corel has announced an SVG plug-in for its CorelDraw (version 9.0) application.

Example of an SVG document

```
<?xml version="1.0" encoding="iso-8859-1"?>
<!DOCTYPE svg PUBLIC "-//W3C//DTD SVG 20000303 Stylable//EN"
"http://www.w3.org/TR/2000/03/WD-SVG-20000303/DTD/svg-
20000303-stylable.dtd" [
  <!ENTITY st0 "font-family:'Verdana';">
  <!ENTITY st1 "font-size:3;">
  <!ENTITY st2 "fill:#FFFFFF;stroke:#999999;">
  <!ENTITY st3 "fill:#FFFFFF;">
                                              .../...
```

```
.../...
  <!ENTITY st4 "fill:#666666;stroke:none;">
  <!ENTITY st5 "font-size:36;">
  <!ENTITY st6 "fill-rule:nonzero;clip-rule:nonzero;
  stroke:#000000;stroke-miterlimit:4;">
    <!ENTITY st7 "stroke:none;">
]>
<svg  width="251pt" height="251pt" viewBox="0 0 251 251"
xml:space="preserve">
  <g id="box_bgd" style="&st6;">
    <path style="&st2;" d="M250.5,250.5H0.5V0.5h250v250z"/>
    <g>
    </g>
  </g>
  <g id="box" style="&st6;">
    <path style="&st3;" d="M231.5,173.5h-205v-102h205v102z"/>
    <text onmouseover="alert('SVG test')"
    transform="matrix(1 0 0 1 29.5 77.5)">
    <tspan x="0" y="0" style="&st7; &st0; &st1;">SVG test
    (small size)</tspan>
  </text>
  </g>
  <a xlink:href="http://www.adobe.com">
    <g id="box_text" style="&st6; &st0; &st5;">
      <text transform="matrix(1 0 0 1 47.5 134.5)">
        <tspan x="0" y="0" style="&st4;">SVG test/tspan>
      </text>
      <text transform="matrix(1 0 0 1 45.5 137.5)">
        <tspan x="0" y="0" style="&st7;">SVG test/tspan>
      </text>
    </g>
  </a>
</svg>
```

This example uses a mixed DTD that contains entities corresponding to (CSS) formatting styles.

The example implements two rectangles and two text zones. The smaller text zone allows you to test the zoom feature and the **onmouseover** action. The larger text zone links to the Adobe Web site.

The main purpose of this example is to demonstrate the quality level obtained when you zoom in.

Here is the result in a browser:

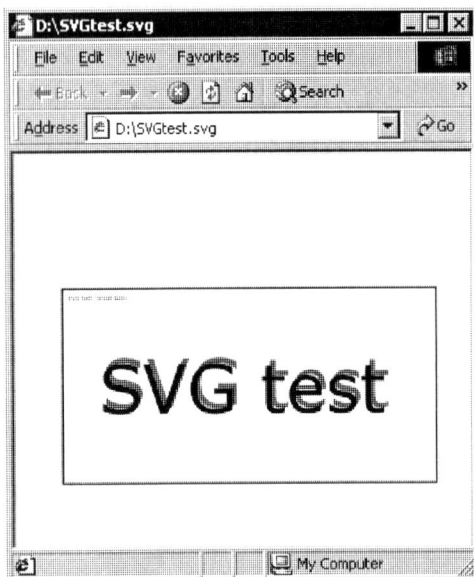

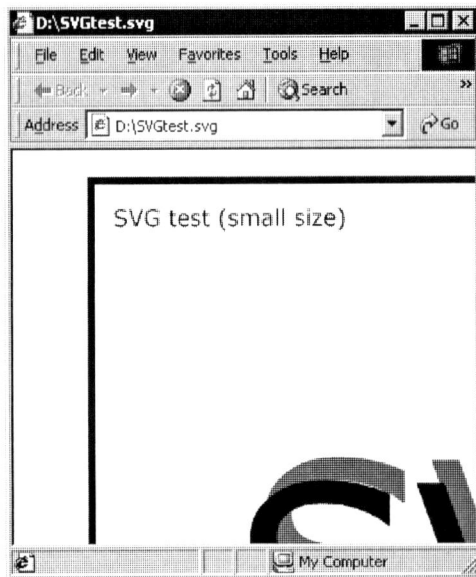

The Appendix of this book contains a more advanced SVG example that uses JavaScript.

> You can obtain further information on this subject from the following Web sites:
> http://www.w3.org/graphics/svg/
> http://www.adobe.com/svg/

2. SMIL

SMIL (Synchronized Multimedia Integration Language) operates in a different multimedia domain than SVG. You can use this language to synchronize different multimedia elements, such as videos, sounds and text. SMIL allows you to create very complex interactive multimedia presentations.

As with SVG, SMIL is an XML application and makes extensive use of XML features. The XML code uses SMIL to specify the behavior of different multimedia objects and how you can interact with these objects via hyperlinks.

A limited number of software resources are available to view the results of this new standard.

You can obtain Java applets that allow you to view a presentation in a browser, for example: HELIO offers the "SOJA Player" and Digital offers HPAS (*Hypermedia Presentation and Authoring System*).

The following multimedia applications also allow you to view the results of these new standards: Microsoft Windows Media Player (version 7.0), Apple Quick Time (version 5.0) and Real Player (version 8.0).

The Oratix company offers a family of multimedia products called GriNS Authoring Software. These programs allow you to create streamed multimedia presentations that you can view with Real Player G2. You can also use these products to create presentations in "pure" SMIL format. These presentations can contain both interactive HTML code and highly complex animations.

A SMIL document contains three parts:

– the first part defines the regions that must receive the different multimedia objects (specifying position and style),

– the second part defines the order and time scale that the objects must follow,

– the third part defines the throughput, according to the type of connection.

Example of a SMIL document

```
<smil>
  <head>
    <!-- Creating the regions in the layout -->
    <layout>
      <!-- root-layout is the main area of your
      presentation -->
      <root-layout height="350" width="600" background-color=
      "#ffffff" title="Pinpoint Positioning"/>
      <!-- regions lay on top of your root-layout: stack them
      with the z-index attribute. -->
      <region id="txtitle" left="10" top="10" height="25"
      width="175" background-color="#ffffff" z-index="2"/>
      <region id="build" left="20" top="30" height="25"
      width="175" background-color="#ffffff" z-index="2"/>
      <region id="1" left="30" top="50" height="25" width="400"
      background-color="#ffffff" z-index="2"/>
      <region id="2" left="30" top="70" height="25" width="400"
      background-color="#ffffff" z-index="2"/>
      <region id="3" left="30" top="90" height="25" width="400"
      background-color="#ffffff" z-index="2"/>
      <region id="finish" left="200" top="170" height="100"
      width="300" background-color="#ffffff" z-index="2"/>
    </layout>
  </head>
  <!-- In the body, fill the regions with images or text and
  apply an execution order -->
  <body>
    <!-- the par synchronisation element determines the running
    order -->
    <par>
      <seq>
        <par>
                                                    .../...
```

Implementing XML

```
.../...
        <text src="media/txtitle.txt" region="txtitle"
        begin="2.00s" end="10s" system-bitrate="14"/>
        <text src="media/build.txt" region="build"
        begin="4.00s" end="10s" system-bitrate="14"/>
        <text src="media/1.txt" region="1" begin="6.00s"
        end="10s" system-bitrate="14"/>
        <text src="media/2.txt" region="2" begin="7.00s"
        end="10s" system-bitrate="14"/>
        <text src="media/3.txt" region="3" begin="8.00s"
        end="10s" system-bitrate="14"/>
      </par>
      <audio src="media/finish.auz" begin="0.01s" end="0.3s"
      system-bitrate="14000"/>
      <img src="media/finish.jpg" region="finish" begin="0s"
      system-bitrate="14000"/>
    </seq>
  </par>
  </body>
</smil>
```

This example describes the build of an SMIL document. First, it displays the title "SMIL example", next it displays "Building a document", then it displays the three phases of building a document, at one-second intervals.

When the program has finished displaying the text, it waits two seconds, removes the text, plays a sound and displays the finish.jpg image to indicate the end of the presentation.

Here is the result in a browser.

Building:

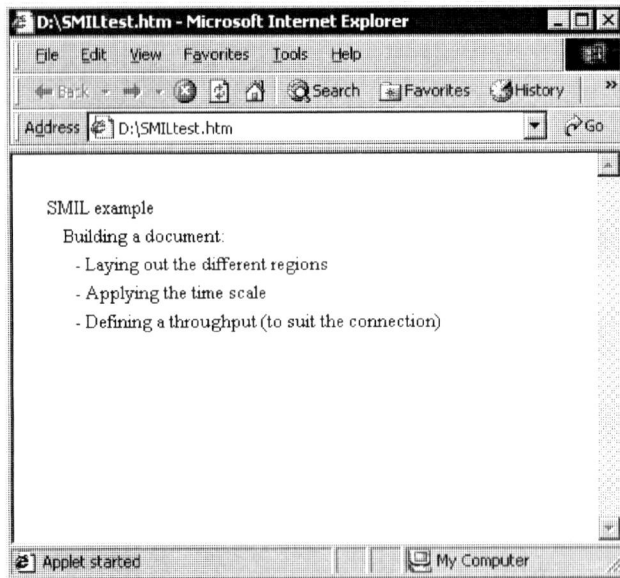

End of the presentation:

Implementing XML

⊙ You can obtain further information on this subject from the following Web site: http://www.w3.org/AudioVideo/.

B. Security

1. XKMS

The purpose of XKMS (*XML Key Management Specification*) is to integrate PKI (*Public Key Infrastructure*) and digital certificates into XML applications. Microsoft, VeriSign and WebMethods developed this standard.

You can use XKMS in your applications for authentication, digital signatures and data encryption. For example, you can use XKMS to validate certificates without needing any proprietary PKI management programs. You can access the various XKMS functions on Web servers using your XML applications.

2. XMLPay

XMLPay is a secure payment application for electronic commerce.

XMLPay provides a wide range of payment methods for B2B (Business To Business) and B2C (Business To Customer) electronic commerce over the Internet (including credit cards and electronic checks).

XMLPay allows you to send payment requests and responses via a secure network. The advantage of XMLPay over other secure payment systems is that it is integrated into the XML work environment.

C. Queries

Relational Database Management System (RDBMS) offer excellent performance and are extensively used in all types of computing architectures. The best-known database query language is SQL. While SQL is a highly effective general purpose query tool, the new XML query standards allow you to query XML document data structures directly (these structures include tags, attributes and data content).

In fact, as the contents of XML documents are irregular and extensible, it is more appropriate to refer to them as semi-structures, rather than structures.

Several XML query languages are being developed at present. You can divide these languages into two categories: languages that process large quantities of data and languages that search the data contents.

XML-QL (*XML Query Language*) belongs to the first of these categories and XQL (*Xml Query Language*) belongs to the second.

As you will have noticed, these two titles have the same meaning. For this reason, these languages are always referred to by their acronyms: XML-QL and XQL (although XQL has not yet been declared as the definitive name for this language).

1. XML-QL

XML-QL must offer the following features:

- It must allow you to express joins.
- It must be simple enough to support existing database query techniques.
- It must allow you to extract data from all existing XML documents and to build new XML documents.
- It must support sorted and unsorted views (although the current XML-QL specification implements only unsorted views).

> You can obtain further information on this subject from the following Web site: http://www.w3.org/tr/note-xml-ql/.

2. XQL

XQL provides an extension to the XSL (XPath) selection language. It uses the Xpath features of identifying node types, indexing and applying filters. This approach makes XQL a simple and powerful tool for running queries.

XQL queries must:

- be concise,
- be easy to understand, easy to create and easy to process with another language,
- be easy to transmit via a URL,
- allow you to extract any type of node or node-set within an XML document (in addition you must be able to select elements via an absolute or a relative path),
- indicate what must be sought and not how it must be sought (this is the role of the query optimizer).

D.Other standards

1. WebDAV

WebDAV (*Web-based Distributed Authoring and Versioning*) is a recent XML-based protocol that is difficult to implement and still under development. WebDAV is an extension to HTTP/1.1. Unfortunately, commands have been added to this protocol that most Web servers do not automatically recognize. For example, Apache requires a patch to support these commands. On the other hand, Windows 2000 Server provides IIS 5 (*Internet Information Server version 5*), which does support WebDAV.

Microsoft's Internet Explorer 5 client also supports this new protocol. It displays servers that support WebDAV, as local folders. This feature allows you to explore these folders, as you would explore local folders, even though they reside on remote HTTP servers.

WebDAV must:

- display object properties (such as the title, author, creation date and any modifications made),
- manage document collections (sets of documents that inherit the same properties),
- share and lock documents to allow several users to work on the same files and to merge any modifications made,
- allow standard operations on objects (such as copying, moving, renaming and deleting),
- allow file access control,
- provide version management.

⊙ Microsoft has integrated this protocol partially in its Office 2000 suite and totally in its Office XP suite. This approach allows you to work directly online with documents that reside on remote HTTP servers.

⊙ You can obtain further information on this subject from the following Web site:
http://www.webdav.org

2. MathML

MathML (*Mathematical Markup Language*) allows you to publish on the Web, scientific documents that contain mathematical equations and formulas. Before the appearance of this language, you had to provide mathematical formulas on the Web in the form of image files.

By associating XML and HTML, MathML allows you to define much more intuitively, not only such formulas but even complex mathematical structures.

This approach will help scientists and engineers to exchange their work via the Web: it will allow them to work directly with each other's formulas using cut-and-paste techniques.

At present, you must represent formulas in the form of images (or in the form of tables, using the H^EV^EA program with HTML3.2). However, neither of these formats allows you to extract the formulas.

Rather than working directly with MathML, it will certainly be much more convenient to use this language at first via translators or automatic generators.

Unfortunately, most browsers (including Netscape, Internet Explorer and Opera) do not manage MathML. Amaya is the only browser that provides any support for this language: it recognizes common symbols but limits your usage of them.

MathML provides different types of element: presentation elements, content elements and the interface.

Presentation elements concern items you can view, such as fractions, indexes or rows in a matrix.

Content elements concern operations that assign variables directly, such as additions.

The interface or "document element" is at the highest level and indicates the start and end of MathML mode.

Example of an absolute value

```
<math xmlns="http://www.w3.org/1998/Math/MathML">
  <apply>
    <abs/>
    <ci>x</ci>
  </apply>
</math>
```

Here is the result in a browser: $|x|$

Example of a factorial

```
<math xmlns="http://www.w3.org/1998/Math/MathML">
  <apply>
    <factorial/>
    <ci>n</ci>
  </apply>
</math>
```

Here is the result in a browser: $n!$

Example of a matrix

```
<math xmlns="http://www.w3.org/1998/Math/MathML">
  <matrix>
    <matrixrow>
      <cn> 0 </cn>
      <cn> 1 </cn>
      <cn> 0 </cn>
    </matrixrow>
    <matrixrow>
      <cn> 0 </cn>
      <cn> 0 </cn>
      <cn> 1 </cn>
    </matrixrow>
    <matrixrow>
      <cn> 1 </cn>
      <cn> 0 </cn>
      <cn> 0 </cn>
    </matrixrow>
  </matrix>
</math>
```

Here is the result in a browser:

$$A = \begin{pmatrix} 0 & 1 & 0 \\ 0 & 0 & 1 \\ 1 & 0 & 0 \end{pmatrix}$$

▶ You can obtain further information on this subject from the following Web site: http://www.w3.org/Math/.

Implementing XML

Appendices

A. Example of XSL and JavaScript

This XSL document example contains JavaScript code to sort on several conditions.

```xml
<?xml version="1.0" encoding="UTF-8"?>
<xsl:stylesheet version="1.0"
xmlns:xsl="http://www.w3.org/1999/XSL/Transform">
  <xsl:output indent="yes" encoding="ISO-8859-1"/>
  <xsl:key name="CDs-by-artist" match="cd" use="artist"/>
  <xsl:key name="CDs-by-type" match="cd" use="spec/@type"/>
  <xsl:template match="/">
    <html>
     <head>
        <link rel="stylesheet" type="text/css"
        href="cd_list.css"/>
        <title>CD list</title>
        <script for="window" event="onload">
           <xsl:comment>
               stylesheet = document.XSLDocument;
               source = document.XMLDocument;
               selectField = stylesheet.selectSingleNode(
               "//xsl:for-each/@select");
               sortField = stylesheet.selectSingleNode(
               "//xsl:sort/@select");
               selFieldLabel= stylesheet.selectSingleNode(
               "//div[@id='sel_label']");
               sortFieldLabel= stylesheet.selectSingleNode(
               "//span[@id='sort_label']");
           </xsl:comment>
         </script>
         <script language="javascript">

                                                   .../...
```

```
.../...
          <xsl:comment>
              function selectArtist(artist){
                selectField.value="key('CDs-by-artist',
                '"+artist+"')"
                updateSelInfo(artist+" CDs")
                update()
              }
              function selectType(type){
                selectField.value="key('CDs-by-type',
                '"+type+"')"
                updateSelInfo(type+" CDs")
                update()
              }
              function sort(type){
                sortField.value=type
                switch(type){
                  case "artist" : type="artist"
                    break
                  case "spec/@type" : type="type"
                    break
                  default :
                    break
                }
                updateSortInfo("sorted by "+type)
                update()
              }
              function init(){
                selectField.value="key('CDs-by-artist',
                /List.CD/cd/artist)"
                updateSelInfo("All CDs")
                update()
              }
              function update(){
                listing.innerHTML =
                source.documentElement.transformNode
                (stylesheet)
                                                   .../...
```

```
.../...
                }
                function updateSelInfo(selInfo){
                  selFieldLabel.text = selInfo
                }
                function updateSortInfo(sortInfo){
                  sortFieldLabel.text = sortInfo
                }
            </xsl:comment>
        </script>
      </head>
      <body>
        <div id="listing">
          <xsl:apply-templates select="List.CD"/>
        </div>
      </body>
  </html>
</xsl:template>
<xsl:template match="*">
   <xsl:apply-templates/>
</xsl:template>
<xsl:template match="List.CD">
  <table>
    <tr>
      <td>
        <div class="pagetitle">
          <xsl:value-of select="page.title"/>
        </div>
        <hr/>
        <table>
          <tr>
            <col width="190"/>
            <col width="200"/>
            <col/>
          </tr>
          <tr>
            <td>
                                                    .../...
```

```
.../...
                <span class="sel_init" onclick="init()">
                All artists.</span>
            </td>
            <td>
                <select id="sel_cd_type"
                onchange="selectType(this.value)">
                    <option value="nothing">Type of cd ...
                    </option>
                    <option value="Live">Concert</option>
                    <option value="SOUNDTRACK">Soundtrack</option>
                    <option value="Studio">Studio</option>
                    <option value="Compilation">Compilation
                    </option>
                </select>
            </td>
            <td>
                <select id="sort" onchange="sort(this.value)">
                    <option value="nothing">Sort by ...</option>
                    <option value="artist">Artist</option>
                    <option value="title">Title</option>
                    <option value="spec/@type">Type</option>
                </select>
            </td>
          </tr>
        </table>
        <hr/>
      </td>
      <td>
      </td>
    </tr>
  </table>
  <div class="label" id="sel_label">
    All CDs
  </div>
  <span class="label" id="sort_label">
  sorted by artist.
                                            .../...
```

```
.../...
   </span>
   <br/>
   <br/>
   <xsl:for-each select="key('CDs-by-artist',
   /List.CD/cd/artist)">
      <xsl:sort order="ascending" select="artist"/>
      <xsl:apply-templates/>
   </xsl:for-each>
 </xsl:template>
 <xsl:template match="page.title">
   <div class="pagetitle">
      <xsl:value-of select="."/>
   </div>
   <br/>
 </xsl:template>
 <xsl:template match="cd">
   <xsl:apply-templates/>
 </xsl:template>
 <xsl:template match="artist">
   <div class="artist">
      <xsl:if test="../spec[@type='SOUNDTRACK']">Soundtrack
        <xsl:if test=".!=''">
           <br/>composed by: </xsl:if>
      </xsl:if>
      <xsl:if test=".!=''">
        <span class="sel_artist"
        onclick="selectArtist('{.}')">
           <xsl:value-of select="."/>
        </span>
      </xsl:if>
      <xsl:if test="../spec[@type='Live']"> in Concert</xsl:if>
   </div>
   <xsl:choose>
      <xsl:when test=".='Keith Jarrett'">Pianist</xsl:when>
      <xsl:otherwise/>
   </xsl:choose>
                                                   .../...
```

```
.../...
  </xsl:template>
  <xsl:template match="title">
    <div class="title">
       <xsl:value-of select="."/>
    </div>
    <xsl:value-of select="../spec/@nb_cd"/> CD
    <xsl:if test="../spec[@nb_cd>1]">s</xsl:if>
    <br/>
    <br/>
  </xsl:template>
</xsl:stylesheet>
```

B. Example of SVG and JavaScript

This example represents a clock.

The example uses JavaScript to manage the hands of the clock.

```
<?xml version="1.0" encoding="iso-8859-1"?>
<svg onload="Init(evt)" width="124" height="124">
  <defs>
    <script language="Javascript">
        function SetTime() {
            var Now = new Date();

            var Seconds = Now.getSeconds();
            var Minutes = Now.getMinutes() + Seconds / 60;
            var Hours = Now.getHours() + Minutes / 60;
            var Year= Now.getYear();
                                                    .../...
```

```
.../...
            if (Year &lt; 2000) {
                Year += 1900;
            }

            SVGDocument.getElementById("seconds").setAttribute
            ('transform', 'rotate(' + (Seconds * 6) + ')');
            SVGDocument.getElementById("minutes").setAttribute
            ('transform', 'rotate(' + (Minutes * 6) + ')');
            SVGDocument.getElementById("hours").setAttribute
            ('transform', 'rotate(' + (Hours * 30) + ')');
            SVGDocument.getElementById("day").getFirstChild().
            setData(Now.getDate()+'/'+(Now.getMonth()+1)+'
            /'+Year);
        }

        function Init(LoadEvent) {
            SVGDocument = LoadEvent.getTarget().
            getOwnerDocument();
            SetTime();
            window.SetTime = SetTime;
            setInterval ("window.SetTime()", 1000);
        }
    </script>
    <path id="outcircle" d="M -46 0 C -46 -63 46 -63 46 0"/>
</defs>
<rect style="fill:#3E5255;" width="124" height="124"/>
<g transform="translate(62 56)">
    <g>
            <circle cx="0" cy="-40" r="3"
            style="fill:white;stroke:white"/>
            <circle cx="0" cy="-40" r="2"
            style="fill:white;stroke:white"
            transform="rotate(30)"/>
            <circle cx="0" cy="-40" r="2"
            style="fill:white;stroke:white"
            transform="rotate(60)"/>
                                                     .../...
```

```
.../...
            circle cx="0" cy="-40" r="3"
            style="fill:white;stroke:white"
            transform="rotate(90)"/>
            <circle cx="0" cy="-40" r="2"
            style="fill:white;stroke:white"
            transform="rotate(120)"/>
            <circle cx="0" cy="-40" r="2"
            style="fill:white;stroke:white"
            transform="rotate(150)"/>
            <circle cx="0" cy="-40" r="3"
            style="fill:white;stroke:white"
            transform="rotate(180)"/>
            <circle cx="0" cy="-40" r="2"
            style="fill:white;stroke:white"
            transform="rotate(210)"/>
            <circle cx="0" cy="-40" r="2"
            style="fill:white;stroke:white"
            transform="rotate(240)"/>
            <circle cx="0" cy="-40" r="3"
            style="fill:white;stroke:white"
            transform="rotate(270)"/>
            <circle cx="0" cy="-40" r="2"
            style="fill:white;stroke:white"
            transform="rotate(300)"/>
            <circle cx="0" cy="-40" r="2"
            style="fill:white;stroke:white"
            transform="rotate(330)"/>
            <text x="-50" y="-45" style="font-family: Arial,
            Helvetica, sans-serif;font-size: 10pt;font-weight:
            bold;color: #5A7377">
              <textPath xlink:href="#outcircle" style="letter-
              spacing:4.5;">
                 <a xlink:href="http://xmlfr.org/index/object.
                 title/SVG/">made with SVG</a>
              </textPath>
            </text>
                                                    .../...
```

```
.../...
    </g>
    <g id="hours" style="stroke-width:2;stroke:#AA1717;
    fill:#AA1717">
            <circle cx="0" cy="-30" r="3">
              <animateTransform attributeName="transform"/>
            </circle>
            <line x1="0" y1="0" x2="0" y2="-30">
              <animateTransform attributeName="transform"/>
            </line>
    </g>
    <g id="minutes" style="stroke-width:2;stroke:#AA1717;
    fill:#AA1717">
            <circle cx="0" cy="-40" r="3">
              <animateTransform attributeName="transform"/>
            </circle>
            <line x1="0" y1="0" x2="0" y2="-40">
              <animateTransform attributeName="transform"/>
            </line>
    </g>
    <g id="seconds">
            <line x1="0" y1="10" x2="0" y2="-50"
            style="stroke-width:1;stroke:white">
              <animateTransform attributeName="transform"/>
            </line>
    </g>
    <g>
            <text id="day" x="-28" y="57" style="color:white;
            align:center;font-family: Verdana, Arial,
            Helvetica, sans-serif;">01/01/2000</text>
    </g>
    <g>
            <circle cx="0" cy="0" r="3" style="fill:white;
            stroke:white"/>
    </g>
  </g>
</svg>
```

A

B

Implementing XML

C

Cascading Style Sheets
    See CSS
CDATA section, *30, 43*
Client-side XML, *182*
Comments, *26*
CorelDraw, *240*
CSS, *61*
    See also Style sheets

D

Data Island, *192*
Data Source Object
    See DSO
Declarations, *23*
Document element, *22*
    See also Elements
Document instance, *9*
Document Object Model
    See DOM
Document summary, *9*
Document Type Definition
    See DTD
DOM, *180, 223*
    appendChild, *228*
    asChildNode, *229*
    attr object, *233*
    ATTRIBUTE_NODE, *224*

E

Entities, *29*
    declaring, *49*
    definable entity, *49*
    external entity, *53*
    internal entity, *53*
    non-parsed entity, *51*
    parsed entity, *51*
    predefined entity, *51*
eXtensible Stylesheet Language
    See XSL

F

FPI (Formal Public Identifier), *35*

H

HTML (HyperText Markup Language), *7, 9*

I

IBM, *7*
IIS 5 (Internet Information Server 5), *250*
Internet Explorer 5 browser, *66*
ISO 9070 standard, *35*
ISO-8859-1 standard, *24*

J

L

M

N

O

P

R

S

start_element, *235*
See also PHP and SAX
Scalable Vector Graphics
See SVG
Server-side XML, *204*
SGML, *7 - 8*
Simple API for XML
See SAX
SMIL, *243*
Standard Generalized Markup Language
See SGML
Standards
multimedia, *239*
Other, *250*
Structure of an XML document, *21*
Style sheets, *61*
summary example, *147*
See also CSS
SVG, *36, 239*
SVG and JavaScript (example), *262*
Synchronized Multimedia Integration Language
See SMIL
SYSTEM keyword, *34*

T

Tagging, *14*
Treeview Control, *218*

V

Valid document, *56*
Visual Basic, *217*

W

W3C, *9*
WebDAV (Web-based Distributed Authoring
& Versioning), *250*
Well formed document, *56 - 57*
World Wide Web Consortium
    See W3C

X

XKMS, *247*
XML Key Management Specification
    See XKMS
XML-QL (XML Query Language), *249*
xmlinst.exe program, *13*
xmlns (XML namespace), *70*
XMLPay, *247*
XPath, *157*
    *, *165*
    */elt, *166*
    ../@att, *166*
    .//elt, *166*
    /, *163*

Implementing XML

List of available titles in the IT Resources Collection

Visit the Internet site for a list of the latest titles published:
http://www.eni-publishing.com

Access 2002 VBA : Programming Access

Implementing XML : Managing and Formatting data

TCP/IP on Windows 2000

Windows 2000 Professional

Windows 2000 Server